David Goodwin
801-426-9579

THE LAST DAYS UNSEALED

AN EXAMINATION OF THE FIVE MAJOR EVENTS OF THE LAST SEVEN YEARS WHICH COVER THE LAST 42 MONTHS OF THE SIXTH SEAL AND FIRST 42 MONTHS OF THE SEVENTH SEAL

By

Robert J. Smith

THE LAST DAYS UNSEALED
By: Robert J. Smith
First Edition

ISBN 1-888106-81-6

Library of Congress Catalog Card Number 99-62477

The views expressed herein are solely those of the author.

Cover Design: Bryan Baker
Cover Art: Bill Kuhre

Printed in the United States of America by

Agreka™ Books

800 360-5284
www.agreka.com

Contents

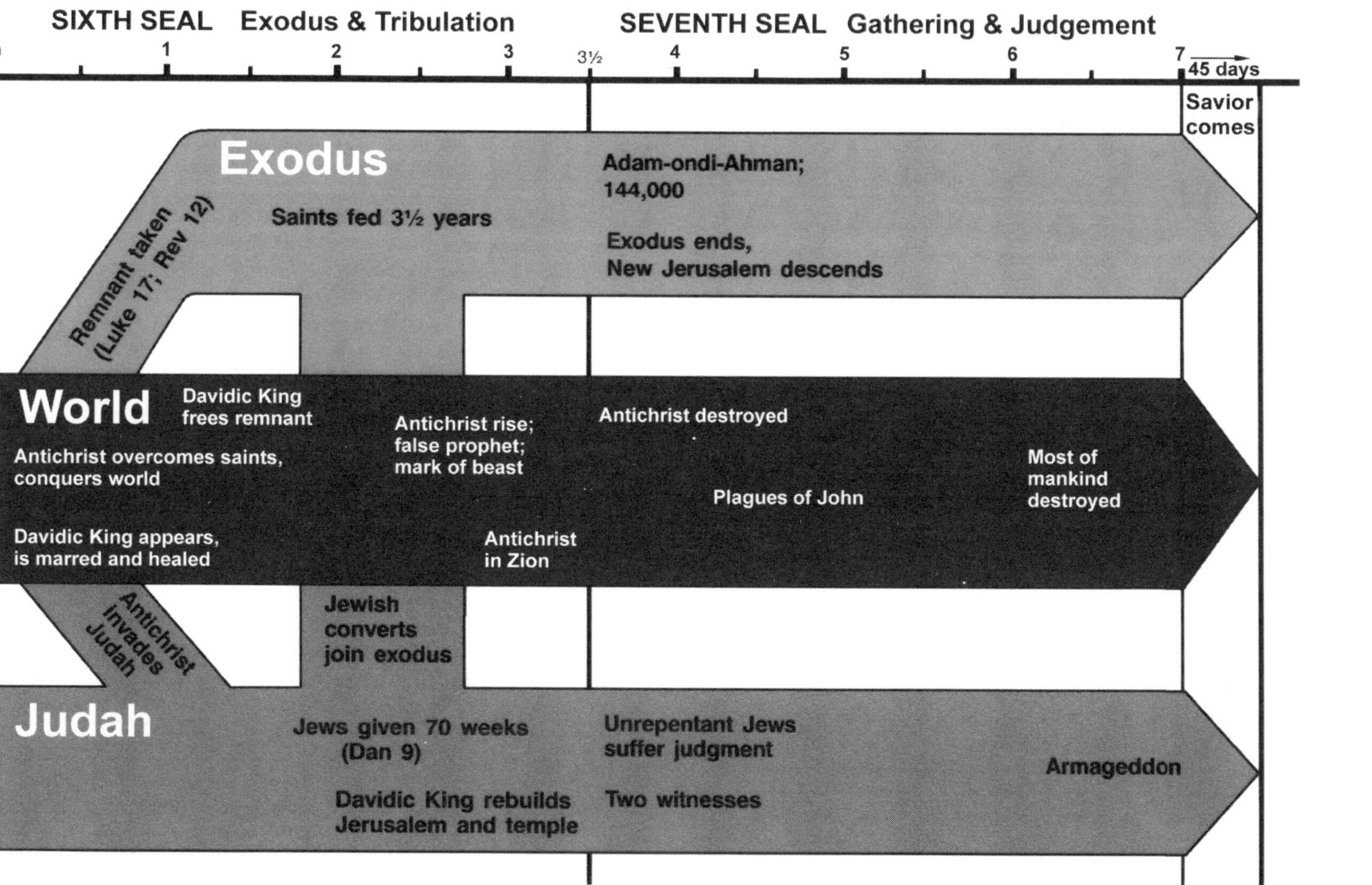
SIXTH SEAL
Exodus & Tribulation
SEVENTH SEAL
Gathering & Judgement
0
1
2
3
3½
4
5
6
7
45 days
Savior comes
Exodus
Remnant taken (Luke 17; Rev 12)
Saints fed 3½ years
Adam-ondi-Ahman; 144,000
Exodus ends, New Jerusalem descends
World
Davidic King frees remnant
Antichrist overcomes saints, conquers world
Davidic King appears, is marred and healed
Antichrist rise; false prophet; mark of beast
Antichrist in Zion
Antichrist destroyed
Plagues of John
Most of mankind destroyed
Antichrist invades Judah
Jewish converts join exodus
Judah
Jews given 70 weeks (Dan 9)
Davidic King rebuilds Jerusalem and temple
Unrepentant Jews suffer judgment
Two witnesses
Armageddon

Introduction

Recently there has been increased interest in the scriptures and prophecies relating to the events immediately preceding the second coming of the Lord in glory. Most feel that we are, indeed, in the final few years or even months in which the prophesied signs and wonders will begin to unfold. This feeling evokes the desire to know more about the things that are soon to happen and these events are the subject of many conversations among church members. As a result of this interest, many books have appeared dealing with last days events.

The question that must immediately come to the reader's mind is, "Why another book on the last days?" I hope the answer to this question will become apparent as you read on. I did not wish to jump on the bandwagon with yet another compilation of some of the last-days scriptures, which most of the books on this subject turn out to be. Nor do I merely wish to rephrase the opinions and ideas that have been floating around the LDS Church for a century or more. After reading all of them as they appear in bookstores, I am a little frustrated that none has very much to offer.

Most of the authors, to be sure, have done their homework as far as researching all of the statements by so-and-so in 1879 and by various general authorities over the years who were expressing their *opinions*. The major verses from D&C are dutifully listed and they include a compendium of quotes from the Bible and the Book of Mormon. There is a little speculation by each about what this prophecy or that prediction may mean, and for the most part, there is nothing new or exciting. What they all, without exception, have in common, is a lack of reference to and understanding of the scriptures that really detail the five major events of the last three-and-one-half years of the sixth seal and the first three-and-one-half years of the seventh seal, or in other words, the last seven years before the Savior returns in glory.

These major events are not only revealed in various scriptures, but the times and order of their occurrence are also given in careful and literal detail. The problem has been the difficulty in understanding these important scriptures, especially Isaiah, the most difficult of all the books to understand, followed by Revelation and then the last half of the Book of Daniel. Nor are we the only ones who have had difficulty with these books. Nephi explained that his own people had trouble with Isaiah:

> *Now I, Nephi, do speak somewhat concerning the words which I have written, which have been spoken by the mouth of Isaiah. For behold, Isaiah spake many things which were hard for many of my people to understand; for they know not concerning the manner of prophesying among the Jews.* (2 Nephi 25:1)

So according to Nephi, there is some specialized knowledge which he calls "the manner of prophesying among the Jews" that must be learned in order to understand what Isaiah is saying as he further explains:

> *...and I know that the Jews do understand the things of the prophets, and there is none other people that understand the things which were spoken unto the Jews like unto them, save it be that they are taught after the manner of the things of the Jews.* (2 Nephi 25: 5)

He goes on to explain that in the very last days men would understand Isaiah:

> *...nevertheless, in the days that the prophecies of Isaiah shall be fulfilled men shall know of a surety, at the times when they shall come to pass. Wherefore, they are of worth unto the children of men,...for I know that they shall be of great worth unto them in the last days; for in that day shall they understand them;...* (2 Nephi 25:7-8)

Nephi tells us two important things here: First men will know of a surety when the prophecies are fulfilled. This has not yet happened, obviously, so their fulfillment, except for a few things, are in the future. The second thing he tells us is that the words of Isaiah will be of great worth in the last days, therefore, the words of Isaiah pertain to the last days. By "last days" I mean, as does Nephi, the very last seven years and not the entire dispensation, although he does talk about conditions at the time when the prophecies *begin* to be fulfilled.

When the Savior appeared to the Nephites following his resurrection, he admonished them to read this one book:

> *And now behold, I say unto you, that ye ought to search these things. Yea, a commandment I give unto you that ye search these things diligently; for great are the words of Isaiah. For surely he spake as touching all things concerning my people which are of the house of Israel;...And all things he spake have been and shall be, even according to the words he spake.* (3 Nephi 23:1-3)

Isaiah is the only book the Lord specifically commanded us to search diligently, yet so few understand it. It is a test of faith for those who truly attempt to fathom the highly metaphorical language and types he uses to picture Israel or the church in the last days. But some of us have diligently searched the words. In addition, the Lord has sent great men among us who have taught us the manner of prophesying of the Jews enabling thousands to understand his marvelous prophecies. This understanding also allows us to more fully understand the other prophets and the ancient books that detail these great events—both good and terrible—and they are now opened to our understanding. But without this understanding, the book is a mystery and so are the wondrous works of which he speaks. All Isaiah quotations in this work are from the Gileadi translation, which is the only correct and understandable translation in the world today.

There are *major* and *minor* events to take place in the last times. Unfortunately, we often dwell on the minor things as signs for which we should be watching. For example, we are expecting that sometime before the Coming, the missionaries will be called home. But what would cause the missionaries to be called home? They will continue to work until world conditions become such that the church cannot safely allow missionaries into the various countries, hence a major event is the condition that causes the existing missionary program to end. Many people look for this as a preliminary sign when in reality, it occurs after something bad has already happened.

Another sign the people watch for is the building of the temple in Jerusalem and the return of the Jews to the land called Israel today. This is again thought to be a preliminary sign but Daniel tells us that the temple will be built in troublous times. So once again something bad is happening before the temple is built.

A commonly held idea is that at some point there will be a large number of people called to go back to Jackson County to build the temple and city. It is thought by some that this will be done while things are going along as they are today. The Lord, however, has assured us that the land of Zion must be redeemed by the shedding of blood and by violence. This means that the inhabitants of that land will have to be removed by war or some catastrophe so the call to go and build, if there is such a thing, will have to come after the violent redemption of Zion.

The point here is that people are waiting for the preliminary signs to occur before they really start to worry or to do much preparation for the coming destruction. When the various signs start to appear, they believe there will be time enough to prepare for the great and terrible day of the Lord. The problem with this thinking is that when the above mentioned and the other commonly believed signs appear, some big-time bad things will have already happened and it will be too late to complete or even begin any preparations. These signs will be discussed in detail hereinafter.

Another idea that is prevalent in our minds is that the coming tribulation and judgments will somehow pass us and affect only the wicked, whoever they are. In spite of the many warnings that the Saints will hardly survive; that the beast will have power to make war with the saints and to overcome them; that Ephraim will be made captive and their dead lie in the streets, this erroneous thinking prevails. The saying that the great and terrible day of the Lord will be "great for the righteous [us] and terrible for the wicked" is often heard. In reality, it will be terrible for everyone, although far worse for some. John hints that many who refuse to take the mark of the beast will be beheaded and millions will die as a result.

The many myths about the last days tend to lull the people into a sense of false security. They also think that because we have a living prophet, we will be warned when the tribulation is about to come so all we need to do is wait for him to give us the word. Again, the trouble with this rationale is that the Lord has already told us all he intends and this is made clear in Isaiah. We have been warned by the many scriptures we have and there will be no more, he says. He told his apostles when he was with them that his coming would be like the days of Noah or the days of Sodom. The people would be marrying, working, and generally going about their business as usual until the fatal day and then it would too late. And this brings up another interesting dichotomy; when the Lord refers to his coming, he does not mean the same thing as we usually do. When we talk about the second coming, we are usually thinking of his coming in glory at which time the tribulation and judgments will have passed. But he refers to his coming as the time of the beginning of trouble. This is also discussed in the book.

In the many books which are available on this subject, none debunks the above false ideas. In fact, if anything, they further perpetuate them. My purpose for writing this work is to describe the major events of the last days and show their time line. The righteous people of the church need to know what lies ahead and something about the time line and order of occurrence of the major events. In this book, I have divided the chapters into chronological chapters as nearly as possible to the order in which the five major last-days events occur. I have chosen to call them *Acts* because this last seven years is like a huge drama which will play out in a very brief period. By the end, the billions of inhabitants of the earth including all sea life, will have been eliminated leaving only a relatively small remnant. Death and destruction of this magnitude is beyond human comprehension. The Lord through Isaiah has said, speaking of our time, that few of mankind would remain and that mankind would be as scarce as the gold of Ophir. This will all take place in a seven-year span. If the world has about 5.5 billion people and only a small remnant will survive, most of this number will then perish. This means that an average of about two-and-a-quarter million people will die each day. That is 2,250,000 people daily. All people of a telestial order, which is most of the population of the world, will have to leave before the Millennium. It seems most important, then, to know how to prepare and survive the coming annihilation of most of mankind.

By heeding the warnings, doing the proper things and ceasing to do the things that are bringing the punishment, we can be spared from most of the worst calamities. But most people in the church do not even realize where we have gone astray. *This book, therefore, purports to be a sort of survival manual for the righteous.* As such, I have not emphasized the general commandments of the church and personal righteousness since these are pretty well understood and personal righteousness is essential to our survival. The purpose of this work is to discuss the events of the last days and not to define what personal righteousness is nor to preach about it. There are major sins, however, that are general and pertain to the church or to Ephraim as a people, and which are the cause of the coming captivity and trouble. These are discussed in detail in the first chapter and elsewhere because they are relevant to the last days scenario.

It is my sincere desire that this book accomplish two purposes: First, I would like to provide information and some comfort to those who are pretty well where they should be in their lives. The most important purpose, though, is to provide the information necessary to assist you in your last minute preparations by providing the correct information about what is about to befall us. If you prayerfully study the exegeses in these chapters, it will change the direction of your life and you will set aside those things that may be placing you in mortal danger.

Chapter I

Setting the Stage

The first of the five great events of the last days is not so much an event as it is a condition or ongoing process. This event is not even talked about by most writers of the last days, yet it is one of the primary themes of Isaiah. Perhaps the reason it is not discussed much is that it is not perceived or realized by most Latter-day Saints. In addition, those who are aware do not want to say too much about these things because it might get them into trouble. The main location for such discussion today is the Internet where many sites are found where one can talk and exchange ideas while remaining relatively invisible. But everyone is conscious that there will be great tribulation, war, pestilence and destruction in the world at some time, but most members are under the impression that it will pass by the church, or at least it will spare the righteous members, whoever they are. Due to this avenue of thought, the real cause of the tribulation is not noticed.

Isaiah begins his book by addressing the church, which he calls Israel. Israel is the name of the ancient northern kingdom which was headed by Ephraim and that kingdom was also often called Ephraim because it was Ephraim who ruled. The Jews today mistakenly call their nation Israel when it is really Judah. But the Lord, through Isaiah, correctly addresses modern Ephraim or Israel which is the church to whom Isaiah is speaking. Throughout this work we must remember that Isaiah is speaking to us, Ephraim, or the church today. He does not address the gentile peoples at all and when he refers to Judah, it is evident. In the introduction, the words of Nephi were quoted (2 Nephi 25:1, 5, 7-8) which show that the prophecies of Isaiah are strictly latter-day events and will be fulfilled in our time. Often we conveniently parcel the good and bad prophecies out; the bad to former times and the good to us and our time. This is wrong. All the prophecies of Isaiah pertain to us today.

Isaiah begins his scathing description of modern Ephraim:

> *Hear, O heavens! Give heed, O earth! The Lord has spoken: I have reared sons, brought them up, but they have revolted against me. The ox knows its owner, the ass its master's stall, but Israel does not know; my people are insensible. Alas, a nation astray, a people weighed down by sin, the offspring of wrongdoers, perverse children: they have forsaken the Lord, they have spurned the Holy One of Israel, they have lapsed into apostasy.* (Isaiah 1: 2-5)

So there it is! The Lord accuses us of lapsing into apostasy. This is a difficult fact for members of the church to accept, but we read it there in black and white. We are like the Jews at the time of Lehi. They had the gospel as it existed at that time, and obeyed the Law of Moses, nevertheless, God sent prophets among them to call them to repentance and to take the course that would have saved them from the Babylonian captivity. Lehi received a revelation that the city of Jerusalem had been destroyed and the people taken captive. Previous to this, however, when they were still in the wilderness, Laman and Lemuel, along with the daughters of Ishmael, wanted to return to Jerusalem. They said:

> *Behold, these many years we have suffered in the wilderness, which time we might have enjoyed our possessions and the land of our inheritance; yea, and we might have been happy. And we know that the people who were in the land of Jerusalem were a righteous people; for they kept the statutes and judgments of the Lord, and all his commandments, according to the law of Moses; wherefore, we know that they are a righteous people; and our father hath judged them, and hath led us away...* (1 Nephi 17:21-22).

Laman and Lemuel, and undoubtedly most of the people at Jerusalem probably looked on themselves as righteous and trying to serve God. But they too had lapsed into apostasy causing the Lord to send them prophets to call them to repentance and warn them of impending calamity.

Today, we do not have a multitude of prophets going about among the people calling us to repentance but we have the scriptures and especially this marvelous book written 2700 years ago specifically for us. Isaiah, in a great cosmic vision, saw our time and the events that would befall. This is the word of the Lord to us. So he tells us that we have lapsed into apostasy and this is a great mystery to most Latter-day Saints because we have the vision that we are righteous, and, like the Jews of Lehi's day according to Laman and Lemuel, are "a righteous people; for they kept the statutes...and all his commandments,...."

We (the active faithful members) attend the temple and would not dream of drinking coffee or tea, not to mention alcohol. We pay our tithes and offerings and attend endless meetings. We hold family home evenings and send our sons and daughters on missions throughout the world. Our devotion is obvious to anyone so who can doubt that we are a righteous people deserving of the Lord's choicest blessings? But there are some things amiss which the Lord points out to us in some rather forthright and graphic terms. The first three chapters of Isaiah spell out the three major sins of the people of the church and the reason for the apostasy. The first of these is idolatry.

Idolatry: The Sin of The Ancients

When the subject of idolatry has arisen in church classes, I have heard many comments that reflect our general misunderstanding of this abomination. The main idea is that idolatry was something our ancestors and pagan peoples indulged in. It involved the worship of idols or gods apart from the true Lord. We are all familiar with the lapses into idolatry of the Israelites throughout their history. They could not leave the worship of the Caananites alone. Since we do not worship any false gods of this sort and do not make idols nor bow down to them, how can we be idolaters? Yet the Lord calls us that. I remember President Kimball calling us an "idolatrous people" a few years ago. (*Ensign*, June 1976)

•Getting Things—The Business of Babylon

Idolatry consists of the making and worshiping of idols. The Lord tells us:

> *O house of Jacob, come, let us follow the light of the Lord. For thou, O Lord, hast forsaken thy people, the house of Jacob, because, like the Philistines, they provide themselves with mystics from the East and are content with the infantile heathen. Their land is full of silver and gold and*

there is no end to their wealth; their land is full of horses and there is no end to their chariots. Their land is full of idols: they adore the works of their hands, things their own fingers have made. (Isaiah 2: 5-8)

The Lord is speaking specifically of his people in this land. We know that it speaks of this land because at the beginning of the chapter, one of the most often quoted scriptures but, unfortunately, not understood until we learned the meaning of the metaphors used here, clearly describes it:

In the latter days the mountain of the Lord's house shall become established as the head of the mountains; it shall be preeminent among the hills, and all nations will flow to it. Many people shall go, saying, Come, let us go up to the mountain of the Lord, to the house of the God of Jacob, that he may instruct us in his ways, that we may follow in his paths. For out of Zion shall go forth the Law and from Jerusalem the word of the Lord. (Isaiah 2:2-3)

This is a prophecy relating to the establishment of this nation, that is, the United States. In the manner of prophesying of the Jews (Isaiah), mountain is a metaphor for nation. If we substitute the word "nation" for "mountain" it begins to make sense. What he is saying is that in the latter days, the nation, wherein the Lord's house would be, would be born. The Lord's house, referred to here, is not the Salt Lake Temple built in the tops of the mountains, as is commonly supposed. The Lord's house, the House of Israel, will be in Jackson County or Zion from where the law will go forth to the world when Zion is established. This nation would become the head of the nations or the most preeminent among them. This has been fulfilled. Much of Ephraim has already gathered to this land and we await the fulfillment of the rest of this prophecy in the next few years, which will be discussed later.

The previously quoted verses further define this land as being full of silver and gold and no end to the wealth. The land is full of horses and chariots, meaning Fords and Toyotas. But he condemns the people of this land because they adore the works of their hands, things their own fingers have made.

The compelling force of wealth and things is that they make us feel good and powerful. One of Satan's great lies is that you can buy anything for money, so the more we have, the more secure we feel. The Lord said that where our treasure is, that is where our hearts will be (Luke 12:34). Wealth makes us proud and arrogant. The Lord goes on:

> *The Lord of Hosts has a day in store for all the proud and arrogant and for all who are exalted, that they may be brought low. He will utterly supplant the false gods. Men will go into caves in the rocks and holes in the ground, from the awesome presence of the Lord... In that day men will throw away to the moles and to the bats their idols of silver and gods of gold which they have made for themselves to adore.* (Isaiah 2:12, 18-20)

The argument against the above charge is that we have not accumulated wealth because we are greedy and seek after these things but rather because the Lord has blessed us with prosperity. As a result, we are worthy of it. With all this wealth we have sent missionaries to the world and have brought millions to a knowledge of the gospel. And this is true, but as the Lord makes clear, our hearts have turned from him and are now set on the things of the world and so this argument and rationalization are not accurate.

People in Utah have become so desirous of wealth, they have allowed themselves to be deceived many times. Utah has the reputation as the scam capital of the country. Every new scam is tried out here. This is the laboratory for confidence games.

In 1987, President Benson issued his inspired counsel to the wives and mothers of the church to stop working and remain home with their children. We have been encouraged to budget our resources so that we can live within our means, whatever they be. Shortly after this injunction was given, there were many disparaging remarks made by men and women both in and out of the church to the effect that "he doesn't understand the situation today." We have convinced ourselves that our wives and mothers have to work and so we send our fair wives off to the Babylonian workplace where they are often subjected to influences and a culture that is abhorrent.

As a people we have enacted legislation that encourages women to enter the work force. Our rulers have enacted laws that set up quotas and preferential policies for women to make it easier to leave home. Women's groups are active in recruiting and soliciting women to run for public office, insisting that there are not enough in office. Most of this action has been brought about by the government but we of the church have accepted it. Yet the Lord has something to say about this:

> *As for my people, babes subject them; women wield authority over them. O my people, your leaders mislead you, abolishing your traditional ways. The Lord will take a stand and contend with them; he has arisen to judge the nations. He will bring to trial the elders of his people and their rulers, and say to them, It is you who have devoured the vineyard; you fill your houses by depriving the needy.* (Isaiah 3:12-14)

He has more to say about our rulers, who are our political leaders, most of whom are also LDS in the Utah area:

> *Your rulers are renegades, accomplices of robbers: with one accord they love bribes and run after rewards;...* (Isaiah 1:23)

It has always been interesting to me to see those who go to Washington to serve for a few years in Congress or other high office. They go as men of ordinary means (although some are wealthy) and return home millionaires. I remember reading of Richard Nixon who went to Congress driving his old Plymouth car. He did nothing but serve in public office and in 1976 when he returned home after resigning, he was a multimillionaire with great investments and estates. This also is the case in Utah and happens to our own rulers, according to the Lord.

There is no doubt that we are guilty as charged. In the past, idolatry has resulted in captivity. The Lord always uses this means to deprive Israel of their idols or their wealth. In captivity, the people become humble again, they repent and the cycle is repeated.

We have established great universities, not so much for the teaching of the humanities: languages, history, arts and letters, but for teaching the means of making wealth. We have opened a law school to teach our young men and women to be lawyers for the purpose of entering Babylon and making lots of money. Our business schools are turning away many applicants—our young people—who want to learn to make money and become wealthy. Success, both in and out of the church, is largely a function of one's income. The wealthy and successful are then called to run the church and to encourage further participation in the Babylonian activities. The business of Babylon is the manufacture and sale of idols. The enticement of the maker/seller/advertiser is that you cannot live without this or that thing. The lust for things becomes our purpose and the love and devotion we should have for our Lord, is lavished on the whore of Babylon. This is what the Lord refers to as committing fornication with the whore, and Ephraim is in bed with her.

•Graven Images—The Gods of the Caananites

The classical form of idolatry, however, is the making of images and bowing down to them. Unfortunately this has become the custom in the church today. In his popular work, *The Last Days*, Avraham Gileadi writes of modern idolatry. (For a complete discussion of this topic, you should read Chapter 1 of this work which is titled "Modern Idolatry—All Is Not Well In Zion.") He says:

> *We are beginning to resemble God's ancient covenant people as they became ripened in iniquity. Indeed, there exist parallels between ancient and modern Israel that provide a yardstick by which we can judge ourselves.* (Gileadi, *The Last Days*, p.9)

It is an amazing phenomenon that we can see so clearly the idolatry of the past but cannot see our own. A few years ago, the president of the church was in Denmark and happened to see the statue of the Christus by Thorvaldsen. The story was retold in the *Ensign* and elsewhere, how he said that this was the closest to the real appearance of the Savior. Permission was granted to copy the statue and bring it here. It now adorns nearly every visitor center of the church.

In the Ten Commandments, in the second of them, the making of graven images and likenesses is forbidden. As far as I know, this commandment has not been repealed. The statue has now proliferated until it is found in our churches and in our homes. Many of the Saints have these statues prominently displayed in their homes. But this is only the tip of the iceberg. The making of statues of Christ is now proceeding apace. The statue of the Christ with the children, the praying Christ and others are now found in every corner. Statues were given as awards in the YW program. This abomination has now captivated the minds of the people.

Along with the widespread use of solid statues, has come an explosion in religious art depicting the Savior. Every issue of the Ensign is now filled with pictures of the Savior and this would seem to be an encouragement to other artists to follow suit. In a recent issue of the Church News, there was a story of a man, in a foreign land, who is marketing T-shirts with images of the Savior printed on them. Once the flood gate is open, the practice is accepted by nearly all and it soon envelops the people of the church. Such pictures are beginning to be displayed in the temples as well.

In ancient times, the Lord referred to the abomination of desolation which consists of placing images in the holy temple. We are now doing that thing. The Christus is being placed in every visitor center which is found near the entrance to the temple. I believe this to be an abomination as the Lord has said repeatedly.

Several years ago, I served a mission in a Catholic country. One of our difficult tasks was to get the new converts weaned from their images. Each home had its shrine with the Virgin Mary, usually, as the central figure of their veneration. A short time ago I was in the home of some friends who are active in the church. As I was leaving, I happened to go in the living room with the man. I was amazed to see a little shrine set up there with, you guessed it, the Christus in the center. I asked my friend about it and he shrugged it off as unimportant and something he did not much want to talk about. Gileadi explains our fascination with images:

> *When we neither see God nor experience him, an image which represents him makes him much more real to us. The image brings him down to our level, limits him to our perception of him. God becomes a concept we can easily deal with, something we can sketch, sculpt, or paint, and mass produce. By adjusting our image of God to mortal notions of him, we manipulate him until the idea of God no longer threatens us.* (Gileadi, *The Last Days*. p.16)

The insidious nature of idolatry is such that we do not perceive its evil at first, but we become comfortable with it and as the images are brought into our homes, they become our household gods just as they were in the homes of the pagans of the past including the home of Abraham's father.

The argument here is not whether or not we have become idolatrous, for that is evident. The question is how long it will be tolerated. Unfortunately, we know the answer which I will discuss further. But graven images, although abominations and very much a part of the church today, are not the only form that is condemned.

•Organized Sports—The Gods of the Olympians

Next to the worship of things is the modern captivity of organized sports. It is amazing how such madness can spread through a civilization. Sports figures are worshiped and paid enormous salaries. We have built huge stadiums where, as is ancient Greece and Rome, the spectacles are presented almost daily and always on the Sabbath. It is not so surprising that this would be the case among the gentiles, but it is quite unseemly for this people. If any does not believe we are similarly infected, he should be in church on a Sunday following a Utah and BYU game, or on Super Bowl Sunday. The brethren can talk of little else and during the football season and especially Super Bowl Sunday, fathers and sons rush home to immerse themselves, together with the rest of pagan gentile America, in the games.

It was interesting that when the basketball player Michael Jordan retired, there was such mourning in this country it was as if the president had been assassinated. The news media showed young girls weeping loudly and inconsolably as if their dearest loved ones had been killed. In fact, people do not mourn this way at the death of a loved one. Gileadi says it this way:

> *So all-consuming have become today's games that they govern many people's thoughts, moods, and actions. In the cause of sports, men may desecrate the Sabbath. Family life may suffer to the point that we hear of "sports widows and orphans." The "next game" may become more important an upcoming event than personal victories in working out our salvation.* (The Last Days p. 29)

To further illustrate this point, let me mention two examples of this abomination among our people. The first is about our young men who attempt to enter the world of professional sports. We have had many young men who have joined professional teams and achieved national recognition. For the most part their lives are exemplary except for one major thing.

The *Church News* covers all such active young men as they

embark on these careers and the implicit official approval is obvious if for no other reason than the coverage in the official church organ. There are stories written praising the many young men who opt to go on their missions before entering professional sports, although other young men by the hundreds of thousands have done so before beginning their life's work. But somehow, these athletes are set apart as something special or of greater achievement.

Recently, a young basketball player was serving his mission. Months before he completed his mission, he was being recruited by the NBA. This was in the press for several months along with excited speculation. Before he completed his mission, he announced that he would play for a certain team who had offered him a contract for nearly $45 million. Upon release from his mission, he began to play for that team and for a year thereafter, he filled the pages of the local sports pages including much coverage in the church press. He was eagerly sought after as a speaker at youth meetings. In all this hoopla, I never heard a negative comment except by some of my associates who are of a like mind. Most approve this since there is no condemnation from the brethren, but rather approval in the church publications.

Let me briefly analyze this with you. Here we have a young man serving in the mission, supposedly calling people to repentance and placing them under covenant to obey the commandments of the Lord and law of the church. One of the commitments of professional sports is that one must perform on Sunday, which is our Sabbath. So one who enters professional sports knows the commitment and that he must be a breaker of his covenant to gain the fabulous salary promised. So this young man, while calling others to repentance, had already made the decision to become a willful and conscious covenant violator. He sold out to Mammon for a seven-year contract worth over $6 million per year.

A prominent LDS author, published a biography of this "great" young man. In the first place, he has not lived long enough to even have a biography, but this shows the inordinate adulation and near worship we accord these people even in the Lord's church. In addition, he has been the speaker at several youth meetings where he is held up as a role model for the young men of the church. There are many others such as him.

Unfortunately, after nearly a year in the NBA, his new masters realized that he was not performing at the level they had expected. The fans became irate and started calling him names such as "The Great White Dope" and "Missionary Impossible" all of which not only brought shame to him but some embarrassment to the church. Even his former bosses, when they announced he had been "sold" to another team, called him a $5.4 million mistake. Apparently that is the amount they paid for his partial-year play.

He was featured in an article in which his address to a large group of young LDS men for "Mormon Night at the Clippers" was reported. The chairman of Mormon Night, said:

> *I was very pleased to hear_____testify of the significance of his mission in his life. He is an Eagle Scout, returned missionary, married in the temple, devoted and loving father, and an outstanding example to our youth. When he spoke to the youth, they listened with rapt attention. He encouraged them to* ***keep the commandments****, go to seminary, listen to their parents and their youth advisers, and plan for missions and temple marriages. He is a great example for our youth."* (*Church News*, Feb. 4, 1995) (Emphasis is mine.)

A few months ago, there was an article in the paper about a young athlete who refused to play professional sports due to play on the Sabbath. He stated that it would be a violation of his covenant which he holds sacred, to play on the Sabbath. One or two athletes have become professional baseball players with the stipulation in their contracts that they not play on Sunday. If they are of enough value to their teams, this is acceptable. But most people do not know of these restrictions. There has been no follow up on the young man who refused to play and I believe most would think him crazy for refusing the deal. This young man was quoted:

> *Several players off 1994 Copper Bowl champion BYU's football team will earn a healthy living for themselves playing football professionally, but offensive tackle Eli Herring isn't one of them. The money Herring would earn as a high draft pick would be welcome—especially since he and his wife, Jennifer, became parents to a daughter 11 months ago. But Herring's principles are: He wants to live the Ten Commandments. Commandment No. 4: "Re-*

> *member the Sabbath day, to keep it holy." To Herring, that means no working—or playing football—on Sunday.* (*Deseret News*, Feb. 15, 1995)

When we see the Bishop for a temple recommend interview, we are asked the basic questions among which is whether or not we keep the Sabbath and attend our meetings and duties. Is the playing of sports on the Sabbath excused on the basis of being in a job that requires one to work on Sunday, such as firemen and policemen? I don't think this is in the same category. It is done to accumulate great wealth and for no other reason. This is fornication with the whore of Babylon. Isaiah has this to say:

> *An oracle concerning the Arena of Spectacles: Whatever is the matter with you, causing you all at once to climb onto the housetops? You resounded with loud cheer—a tumultuous town, a city of revelry! But your slain were not killed by the sword; they did not die in battle! For my Lord, the Lord of Hosts, has in store a day of trampling and riot in the Arena of Spectacles, a day of battering down walls, and of crying in distress, To the mountains!* (Isaiah 22:1-2, 5)

Isaiah is seeing a vision of the last days and wonders "Whatever is the matter with you,..." I have often wondered the same thing. Here he gives us a picture of what will happen to us and he compares it to the rioting and trampling that often takes place today but when this event happens, there will be battering down of walls and people will cry, "To the mountains!"

We have all been captivated by this mania to some degree. In my own ward two or three years ago, the Bishop stood toward the end of Sacrament Meeting and said that it was time to dismiss and he knew that most of us were anxious to get home to watch the Super Bowl. He was not being sarcastic but was serious.

I have to say one more thing about this form of idolatry which shows just how firmly the insanity has the members of the church in its grip. For the past several years Utah, and particularly Salt Lake City, have tried to get the Olympic Games here. In 1995, they were successful and Salt Lake City was selected as the host city for the 2002 Winter Olympic Games. There were exuberant celebrations around the state, particularly in the area surrounding Salt Lake City.

Millions were spent on this effort and after the award, millions more are being committed to build the finest sports facilities and provide housing for the athletes and guests. Suddenly there is unlimited funding for this activity, both from private donations and from public money allocated for it, although it is a private business and any appropriation of public moneys to it is illegal. In polls, with few exceptions, all are in favor of the games and of spending whatever it takes both to win, which was done, and to stage them. The coming games provide two things: a great sports spectacle which we worship, and the chance to make millions of dollars but not for the poor or ordinary citizens. The profit will go to government increasing the power of our rulers over us, and to businesses and individuals who have products and services to sell.

The amazing thing about all this is that many of those who are strongly in favor of the 2002 Olympic Games are our LDS people and leaders. They are acting as nutty as the rest but either their ignorance of the scriptures or their lack of belief in them is the cause. If they were familiar with the scriptures, which will be unfolded later in this book, they would realize that the Olympics will likely never be staged here. If our calendars coincided with the Lord's time table, it would be obvious that the year 2002 is out in the seventh seal. We know we are a little off, but this year is still at the end of this dispensation and it is probable that the tribulation will have begun by then. Even if it does not, we should be putting our resources into preparation for the catastrophe that is about upon us. More about this later.

Injustice: The Sin of King Noah

The next thing the Lord has to say about his people, Ephraim, in the last days is about our failure to provide justice. In a society as people become more affluent, their wealth has to come from some source. True wealth is created by what comes from the ground. This consists of minerals, raw materials and crops which we grow. This wealth brings honorable increase to the person who develops these resources. The farmer labors to raise crops which he then sells or trades for the other things he needs. This works no hardship on anyone. The man who harvests timber likewise uses the resources God has provided for building our homes, making paper and providing fuel for homes, especially in areas where there is no other fuel. The miner harvests the resources of the land to make the useful items required by society. This is the basis for true wealth.

In our modern society, however, men have set up ways to create wealth from nothing or without real resources. This is mainly done through the device of modern banking and speculation based on the Babylonian ideal of greed as the great motivator. In this way, wealth can be created out of nothing. A bank can issue credit, which is nothing. No goods or actual hard money are given. The bank merely says it will give you credit. You then take the credit and secure the "things" you desire but cannot pay for. You then must create wealth from the earth, or work for someone who will pay you for your labor or your combined knowledge and labor. You must take this currency received and pay it to the one giving the credit plus an additional amount for the use of the credit.

By the above method, people can acquire the "things" they desire before they have accumulated the money to pay cash for them. In this way, Babylon gradually places us in bondage to those who give credit. Some argue that this provides a higher standard of living for all and they may be correct, but they create the desire for things which we cannot always satisfy. The natural tendency is to extend ourselves to the limit of our credit. In America today, according to a national economic newsletter, after paying the fixed monthly expenses (housing and utilities) 94 percent of the remaining income is used for debt payment (credit cards, installment payments, etc.) for the average person. I know from the cases of many of my friends, who are mostly members of the church, that they are in this situation with most of their credit cards maxed out. The credit is being largely used to buy nonessential things. Isaiah tells us:

> *Attention, all who thirst; come for water! You who have no money, come and buy food, that you may eat. Come, buy wine and milk with no money and at no cost. Why do you spend money on what is not bread, your labor on what does not satisfy?* (Isaiah 55:1-2)

Isaiah is speaking in the metaphorical sense but also in the material. He is speaking of the bread of life in both senses. The righteous will eat of the free bread, wine and milk, but the admonition he gives in the question, why do we spend our money on that which is not bread, applies to us in the current material sense.

Our labor is mortgaged out to buy the things which do not satisfy. In addition, when we are so financially encumbered, we have no means to help the poor and the needy, the widows and fatherless. This is one of the great condemnations that the Lord holds against us, Ephraim or the church, today.

> *Wash yourselves clean: remove your wicked deeds from before my eyes; cease to do evil. Learn to do good: demand justice, stand up for the oppressed; plead the cause of the fatherless, appeal on behalf of the widow. How the faithful city has become a harlot! She was filled with justice; righteousness made its abode in her, but now murderers. Your silver has become dross, your wine diluted with water. Your rulers are renegades, accomplices of robbers: with one accord they love bribes and run after rewards; they do not dispense justice to the fatherless, nor does the widow's case come before them. I will restore my hand over you and smelt away all your dross as in a crucible, and remove all your alloy....For Zion shall be ransomed by justice, those of her who repent by righteousness.* (Isaiah 1:16-17, 21-23, 25, 27)

The awful sin of greed, which is the stock and trade of Babylon, has caused us to become an unjust people. In that, I mean, as the Lord does in the above quotation, that we have ceased to perform justice for all our people. Our rulers take bribes and sell justice. It has been said that our courts no longer provide justice but that they enforce law and there is a very great difference. The courts are so occupied with litigating matters of great wealth and commerce that the needs of the common people seeking redress and justice are not heard.

The Lord calls our rulers "renegades and accomplices of robbers." We are robbed by exorbitant taxes and other fees but are denied the protections for which we pay. Much of the money is used for things the government is not authorized to do. For example, they set up RDAs, which are simply land grab agencies through which, under color of law, the rulers can condemn and seize the legitimate property of its citizens and force them to leave.

Many who are deeply in debt find that they cannot pay for the things they have bought on credit and they lose them. People are so deeply encumbered to Babylon, that if either the husband or wife loses his job, or if one dies, they lose their home. Our cities teem with homeless and poor. Every day we read of the plight of children in this, the wealthiest of nations, where one in four lives in poverty. Single mother families have reached epidemic proportions with about one third of the children in this country living in single parent homes. Many of these families are in dire poverty. The Babylonian system has no means to take care of them. If they cannot make it in Babylon, it is just too bad.

I do not intend to get into a political discussion here. It is sufficient to say that these people exist and there are many of them in the church. They are not being taken care of adequately and the Lord condemns us for this. This is the sin of King Noah, who began to tax the people and place heavy burdens upon them. He built great public works and magnificent buildings. The Book of Mormon condemns this activity. Finally, King Noah expelled the righteous and humble members of his kingdom. Our society has become precisely like that of King Noah and the poor and humble are suffering. The Lord tells us:

> *He will bring to trial the elders of his people and their rulers, and say to them, It is you who have devoured the vineyard; you fill your houses by depriving the needy. What do you mean by oppressing my people, humbling the faces of the poor? says the Lord of Hosts.* (Isaiah 3:14-15)

So he has pronounced the decree against the leaders of this people, both the elders and rulers, the latter being the political leaders, most of whom are LDS in Utah.

The Sabbath: The Sign Of The Covenant

The third major transgression the Lord calls to our attention at this day, is our Sabbath observance. The Sabbath was instituted as a covenant sign between God and his special covenant people, Israel who is at this time, Ephraim. The world has no regard for the Sabbath except for a few devout Christians, Jews and some others. The Sabbath in America today is a day for fun, recreation, shopping, and of course, for attending professional sports activities. This fever has caught the members of the church as well as the rest of the country.

> *And that thou mayest more fully keep thyself unspotted from the world, thou shalt go to the house of prayer and*

> *offer up thy sacraments upon my holy day: For verily this is a day appointed unto you to rest from your labors, and to pay thy devotions unto the Most High; Nevertheless thy vows shall be offered up in righteousness on all days and at all times; But remember that on this, the Lord's day, thou shalt offer thine oblations and thy sacraments unto the Most High, confessing thy sins unto thy brethren, and before the Lord. And on this day thou shalt do none other thing, only let thy food be prepared with singleness of heart that thy fasting may be perfect, or, in other words, that thy joy may be full.* (D&C 59:9-13)

This is the commandment of the Lord to Israel in the last days as given to Joseph Smith. Isaiah has somewhat to say on this subject as well.

> *Why, when we fast, do you not notice? We afflict our bodies and you remain indifferent! It is because on your fast day you pursue your own ends and constrain all who toil for you. You fast amid strife and contention, striking out savagely with the fist. Your present fasts are not such as to make your voice heard on high. Is this the manner of fasting I have required, just a time for men to torment themselves? Is it only for bowing one's head like a reed and making one's bed of sackcloth and ashes? Do you call that a fast, a day of the Lord's good graces? Is not this the fast I require: To release from wrongful bondage, to untie the harness of the yoke, to set the oppressed at liberty and abolish all forms of subjection? Is it not to share your food with the hungry, to bring home the wretchedly poor, and when you see men underclad to clothe them, and not to neglect your own kin? If you will keep your feet from trampling the Sabbath—from achieving your own ends on my holy day—and consider the Sabbath a delight, the holy day of the Lord venerable, and if you will honor it by refraining from your everyday pursuits—from occupying yourselves with your own affairs and speaking of business matters—then shall you delight in the Lord and I will make you traverse the heights of the earth and nourish you with the heritage of Jacob your father. By his mouth the Lord has spoken it.* (Isaiah 58:3-7, 13-14)

The citations above make it very clear what the Lord expects of us on the Sabbath. I think no further explanation is required, and it is not my purpose to explain these commandments but merely to show that we are not doing what he commands.

In General Conference, Saturday April 6, 1996, Elder Earl Tingey gave an address on the Sabbath with the emphasis almost entirely on shopping. He discussed the widespread practice of the members to shop on this day. The tendency is to adopt the customs and practices of the people among whom we live. The influence of the Babylonian world is so great that we are drawn into the sins of our neighbors.

As we read the stories of ancient Israel, we are appalled that they adopted the customs of the Caananite peoples around them. But we are doing the same things. Nonmembers from other states and countries have come to Utah and brought their customs with them. We are now surrounded by these people in this land we settled. They force the stores to do business on Sunday and they behave the same as do gentiles in other places. We have gradually accepted their customs, dress, actions and in many cases, their value systems. Of course there has been a political move on the part of the church to show the world that we are just like the other Christian churches and just as Christian as they are, by darn! As a result, we have done all we can to cease being a peculiar people and now you cannot distinguish a Mormon from a non-Mormon in our town. We try to blend into the culture of which we are becoming a minority. In addition, the church has hired a PR firm to create an image for the church that will blend in with the Christian world and make us less distinguishable.

Statistics show that about 70 percent in Utah are LDS, but we know from inside, that only about 35 percent of the members of the church are active and that only about 12 to 15 percent have temple recommends at any time. That means that 12 to 15 percent are active LDS, because the requirements for obtaining a temple recommend are the same as for being baptized into the church; the very basic requirements. And 85 percent, after joining the church or after having been lifetime members, cannot or do not wish to adhere to the basic tenets of the church. So the active people who are trying to keep the commandments are in a minority and outnumbered about seven-to-one by gentile types.

Many are even bashful about this activity and try to keep it under wraps so as not to attract attention. This is not so hard to understand either. Many of us have been threatened, including this writer, if we so much as discuss religion in the workplace. The federal government has made "religious harassment" a crime and that is enough to stop anyone with an evangelical bent.

Because of these influences, if we are not vigilant, we find ourselves doing the same things as our neighbors. Our kids want to go with their nonmember friends and it creates a real struggle in the home. Many parents give in thinking they will straighten out when they are older or that they will not be adversely influenced. They will go on missions which will reform them (unless they are professional athletes). But it does not work out that way. They come home with the same customs and habits.

Elder Tingey did not mention professional athletes and the fact that they are willful covenant breakers but perhaps that is because this group of people have an official dispensation to sin. I think that because the sports idolatry is so nearly universal in the church, that the brethren are hesitant to attack this false god or that they are themselves under this spell. Attacking this evil could split the church and obviate all efforts to reactivate the many inactive brethren in the church. Besides one must consider that these millionaire athletes pay millions in tithing and wealth, as we pointed out, covers a multitude of sins, to quote a cliché. In addition, the church has used the sports programs of the church to entice young men to be baptized, such as happened in the 1960s with the notorious baseball conversions. As a result, it may be impossible for the brethren to say anything having painted ourselves into a corner.

The failure to properly observe the Sabbath leads to serious spiritual deterioration and vitality in our services. I have often pondered the fact that I am so bored in the meetings and that they seem to be so bad. After reading what the Lord through Isaiah has to say, I still may feel a little guilty, but I understand my neurosis:

> *When you come to see me, who requires you to trample my courts so? Bring no more worthless offerings; they are as a loathsome incense to me. As for convening meetings at the New Month and on the Sabbath, wickedness with the solemn gathering I cannot approve. Your monthly and regular meetings my soul detests. They have become*

> *a burden on me; I am weary of putting up with them. When you spread forth your hands, I will conceal my eyes from you; though you pray at length, I will not hear...* (Isaiah 1:12-15)

Remember, the Lord is speaking to us. This is not counsel he gave to the people of Isaiah's day. I remember being in a Ward Council meeting and the bishop was discussing the matter of our sacrament meetings. For some time, it had been apparent that our meetings lacked verve. Once, while we were talking about reactivating people, it was suggested, after other steps, that they should be encouraged to start coming to sacrament meeting. *Someone remarked that our sacrament meetings were not of a quality to inspire anyone to spiritual change or activity.*

Our meetings have become noisy, irreverent affairs. It is extremely difficult to meditate even during the sacrament. Children and even adults walk in and out during the passing of the sacred emblems. It is very distressing to me and must be more so to the Lord. This is perhaps what he means by "trampling his courts so." The worthless offerings are no doubt referring to our lack of humble hearts and contrite spirits, which is the sacrifice he requires of us.

About once a month, the sacrament meeting is occupied by a young couple who has moved into the ward. They tell of how they met at BYU and finally got married. They seldom have any message of spiritual significance to the Sabbath and most are repetitive. One meeting a month is provided for the high counselor to speak. He is assigned a message and, depending on his preparation, it can be quite good or not so good. One Sunday, of course, is fast and testimony meeting. The balance of the speakers, on the remaining Sunday, are usually assigned topics by the bishop such as faith, word of wisdom, repentance, or other very basic subjects. There are two or three speakers on the program which means that each only has about 10 minutes and in that time, it is impossible to develop the subject and most are not trained to focus on and treat one aspect. It usually amounts to some quotes on the subject, the usual cliched statements and maybe an example from personal experience.

This is not the fault of the speakers. The church has limited the subject matter which can be addressed. We can not talk about the last days nor the second coming. The instructions from the top are to confine all sermons to the first principles. In addition the speakers are not professional and most are asked to speak only once in several years. In fast and testimony meeting, often the same people speak. But the adults sit in boredom listening to nothing new, chatting with neighbors, playing with kids or sleeping. When the meeting is ended, there is a great unspoken but evident sense of release and the people head for the door, hungry and tired.

There are various reasons for this condition in addition to our collective attitude about the Sabbath and although I have some ideas, it is sufficient to conclude that Sunday is not what it should be making the Lord displeased. He detests our meetings and our Sabbath observance. This fault of the Lord's people, is the final major condition in our apostasy.

These three lapses then—idolatry, injustice and breaking the Sabbath—have set the stage for the calamities which have been promised upon the Lord's people.

America: Setting Up The Tribulation

There are many prophecies about the United States in the last days. Most of these prophecies are found in various books. The best, in fact, the only book I would recommend in addition to Gileadi's works mentioned earlier, is *Prophecy—Key to the Future*, by Duane S. Crowther. This was published about 35 years ago and is still the best compilation of prophecies relating to the last days. The copy I have was reprinted in 1992 and is available in bookstores. It is a good reference work on the topic. What is missing are the prophecies in Isaiah and of course, at that time we could not understand Isaiah. Isaiah has now been unsealed and the balance of this work deals with these newly understood scriptures and others that have been unfolded by our understanding of Isaiah.

Since I and most of you, who may be reading this book, live in the US, and the main body of the church is here, the prophecies relating to the US are very important. Our histories are intertwined and what affects the nation, affects the church. In Isaiah 2:2-3, which is quoted above, the Lord said that the mountain of the Lord's house would be established as the head of the mountains. Note in the correct translation, the term is "head of the mountains." In the KJV it says "in the top of the mountains." This is often misquoted by members "in the tops of the mountains" since this is assumed to be literal. But the meaning is the same in both versions. Mountain is a metaphor for nation so either "head of the nations" or "top (singular) of the nations" makes sense in metaphorical meaning. The top or head mountain, refers to the nation which would become the preeminent nation in the world and here the nation or people of the Lord's house would be established. When analyzed, this is clearly a prophecy of the founding of this nation, the United States, and all nations would flow unto it. This has literally been fulfilled.

The prophecy does not refer to the building of a temple here. It means the nation of the Lord's house, which is the house of Israel. This land has been given to Israel for an everlasting inheritance and is in real fact, the nation of the Lord's house, the House of Israel. I am sorry to have to dispel the erroneous interpretation of these verses, especially since so much money was spent on the film and publicity in 1993 when the 100th anniversary of the Salt Lake Temple was commemorated under the title "The Mountain of the Lord's House." Nevertheless, it is so.

The United States was to become the top or head nation and preeminent among the other nations. This is another convention which the Hebrew prophets used. It is called parallelism. This is the repetition of the same idea using two different terms. So top of the mountains or head of the mountains is parallel with preeminent among the hills meaning the same thing. The United States began to be preeminent following World War I although we were still not considered one of the major nations. During the 20 years following the war, the US became a major industrial nation surpassing the nations of Europe. By the time World War II came along, we were the most economically developed nation in the world.

The free world, especially England, depended on our material output to survive during the first years of the war. We later poured troops into Europe, Africa and the Pacific turning the tide of war and defeating the Axis powers. After World War II, there was no doubt about the superiority of the United States in almost every category. So the fulfillment of this prophecy occurred between 1946 and now. It is a question, however, whether or not the US still retains this status.

In the past few years, we have been in a downward plummet

economically, spiritually, and educationally. We have been shipping our industry overseas at a tremendous rate. There is little heavy manufacturing in the US now except for a few auto factories and a handful of other industries. The electronics industry is in the orient. All TVs come from Japan along with nearly all computers. In the past few years over 3000 factories have relocated to Mexico or other countries as a result of the NAFTA and GATT treaties. This has resulted in millions being laid off.

Government reports that economic growth is great and millions of new jobs have been created. National unemployment is about six percent and all is well with the economy. In a Congressional hearing on employment, which I watched on C-Span, a commission employed by the federal government called the Federal Employment Commission, admitted that the six percent figure is based only on those who apply for unemployment benefits. The spokeswoman who was giving the information said that in reality the figure was about three times as high. In addition, we have people with families who are working at jobs paying $5-to-$10 per hour because they cannot find suitable employment. These people are unemployed because they are not employed in their skills or professions and are not earning a living. These people are not counted. If all the people in these categories are counted, and we count those who have to work two or three jobs to eke out a living, then the figure is much higher and we see unemployment at more like 25 to 30 percent.

I know that this kind of talk is considered unpatriotic and probably politically incorrect but it is true. And these conditions are important because they are the precursors of troubles that are about to erupt in this country. And before I go on with the prophecies, I will remind you that this period, from the restoration of the gospel in 1830 until a point when the gospel will no longer be preached to the gentiles, is called the "times of the gentiles." This is the time when they have the opportunity of receiving the gospel from the missionaries or the church. When the times of the gentiles is fulfilled, the gospel will no longer be preached to them. So we are in that time slot.

We have seen some other conditions of late in this country which are rather scary. We have had massive flooding in many states such as Illinois, Iowa, Indiana and many other states in

1995. The wheat and other crops were severely damaged or destroyed. The following year there was an acute shortage of wheat. In 1995, treated, bagged wheat for home storage was available for about six dollars for 50 pounds. In the spring of 1996 it nearly doubled and was difficult to find. Texas and Arizona had a new disease from Mexico which infected the wheat crops there and a half million acres of wheat had to be burned. The next couple of years were a little better but these crises show how fragile our food supply is. In this decade we have seen very much trouble due to the weather. It would not take much to cause a severe shortage of food. Let's look at some of the prophecies relating to this land:

> *And now I am prepared to say by the authority of Jesus Christ, that not many years shall pass away before the United States shall present such a scene of bloodshed as has not a parallel in the history of our nation; pestilence, hail, famine, and earthquake will sweep the wicked of this generation from off the face of the land, to open and prepare the way for the return of the lost tribes of Israel from the north country.* (DHC 1:315)

> *I saw men hunting the lives of their own sons, and brother murdering brother, women killing their own daughters, and daughters seeking the lives of their mothers. I saw armies arrayed against armies. I saw blood, desolation, fires.* (DHC 3:390-1)

There are many such prophecies given in the early days of the church. Brigham Young, Wilford Woodruff, Orson Pratt, Parley P. Pratt, Heber C. Kimball and many others gave their prophecies of these days and the doom pronounced on this nation. The Lord spoke of this in Isaiah, which has not been understood until now:

> *An oracle concerning Egypt: When the Lord enters Egypt riding on swift clouds, the idols of Egypt will rock at his presence and the Egyptians' hearts melt within them. I will stir up the Egyptians against the Egyptians; they will fight brother against brother and neighbor against neighbor, city against city and state against state. Egypt's spirit shall be drained from within; I will frustrate their plans, and they will resort to the idols and to spiritists, to mediums and witchcraft. Then will I deliver the Egyptians into*

the hand of a cruel master; a harsh ruler will subject them, says my Lord, the Lord of Hosts. The waters of the lakes shall ebb away as stream beds become desolate and dry. The rivers shall turn foul, and Egypt's waterways recede and dry up. Reeds and rushes shall wither; vegetation adjoining canals and estuaries, and all things sown along irrigation channels, shall shrivel and blow away and be no more. Fishermen will deplore their lot and anglers in canals bemoan themselves; those who cast nets on water will be in misery. Manufacturers of combed linen and weavers of fine fabrics will be dismayed. the textile workers will know despair, and all who work for wages suffer distress. (Isaiah 19:1-10)

In this long quote we have a picture of some very serious events to occur very soon. But, you may say, what does this prophecy have to do with us since it is against Egypt? In Isaiah, Egypt is the United States. Isaiah uses types as he says, and Egypt, which was the leading, preeminent and top-of-the-mountains empire at that time is the type of the nation which is preeminent today. The Lord refers to Assyria throughout Isaiah and the king thereof as the great latter-day archtyrant or antichrist. There is no country of Assyria today so this must be some other modern, warlike and powerful nation of whom ancient Assyria is a type. This is Russia today. And now that the players are identified we can look at the details of the prophecy.

In the first verse, Isaiah says the Lord will enter Egypt riding on swift clouds. Clouds are another metaphor which means trouble. This is the beginning of the difficulties that come upon this land. First, the idols will rock at his presence. To rock means to become unsteady. The US stock market is shaky, at unprecedented high levels and the stocks are drastically overpriced and ready to collapse at the slightest crisis. The idols will not be taken so much for granted and will be seen by some to be false gods after all. The people will be afraid and as Isaiah says, their hearts will melt within them. Whatever happens will cause great fear. The question is what can cause such consternation?

Whatever happens is going to make people angry with one another and even go to war with each other. This is not going to be a civil war such as we had before where the country was divided into two groups. This war or disturbance will cause individuals, even fathers and sons, and mothers and daughters to fight. But cities will fight against other cities and even states will fight against states and the country will be demoralized and unable to react as a nation. The unity of the country will be gone. The will to fight will likely be sapped as well.

What could cause such an eruption? I discussed above the conditions in this country at this point in history. There are other factors at work as well. There are many groups in this country who are angry at the government or at other people and groups.

The American Indians are one such group. We do not hear much about them but they have been trying for several years to compel the government to honor the treaties made with their people more than 100 years ago. They want their lands restored to them. Representatives of all the North American tribes have met to discuss their options and violent rebellion has not been ruled out, according to my source of information.

Another group which is becoming very active are the Blacks. There are elements among them who are trying to arouse feeling of animosity against whites for past injustices. Some of these groups are demanding reparations in the hundreds of billions and the turning over to them of five Southern states for the establishment of a country called New Afrika. One Black Leader has traveled to Libya, Sudan and elsewhere, contrary to the orders of the government, to raise funds for this cause. Their speeches are most militant and they are calling for whatever it takes, including violence, to get their desires satisfied.

There is a strong patriot movement in this country composed of various groups and philosophies. Some are religious, such as the Branch Davidians and others are strictly secular. Militia groups have formed in nearly every state, with some having as many as 30,000 members. The major ones have been in the news such as the Michigan Militia which is one of the biggest and the Montana Militia which is not only large, but has its own media outlets. These groups are suspicious of the government and with good reason. In turn, the government perceives them as potential threats and possible terrorists.

This prophecy is quite comprehensive and does not mention any groups as being the instigators of the civil chaos. In verses 5-

7 the problems seem to be related to the weather. Isaiah says the waters ebb away and stream beds dry up. One could possibly make a case that he is speaking metaphorically and that the waterways and streams are people. Moving water usually means moving people or an army. But that this is not the case is made clear in verses 8-10. There the fishermen are in misery because there is no water and people are out of work. This is a major depression.

Historically, the only thing that has caused people to kill each other, especially fathers and sons, mothers and daughters, is famine. In times of famine, people will kill and eat their own children. The vegetation is drying up and blowing away, he says. This is a description of drought. If there is a drought, there will be no crops. Early in the spring of 1996 there was great flooding. There was serious danger of massive crop failures, which in fact did occur but there was enough to keep us going. But a similar catastrophe could result in the only scenario I can see as probable to fit this situation, but there are two different ways to set it off.

If there were a drought or other weather phenomena which caused the crops to be destroyed, it would trigger immediate panic. There is a prophecy in D&C 29:16 which tells of a hailstorm sent to destroy the crops of the earth, but in context, this happens during other events which in turn happen at a specific time in the future. The problem is not the great hailstorm then. The cause has to do with food and it does not matter what causes the shortage. We were briefly, however, in the midst of a food shortage in this country with the destruction of our grains due to flooding and disease in 1995 and 1996.

> *Even now, the Lord, the Lord of Hosts, deprives Judea and Jerusalem of both staff and crutch—all food supply and water supply, ...* (Isaiah 3:1)
>
> *Up, and listen to my voice, O complacent women; you careless daughters, hear my words! In little more than a year you shall be in anguish, O carefree ones, for when the harvest is over, the produce shall fail to arrive.* (Isaiah 32:10-11)

When the food is unable to be delivered and is in short supply, states and cities who have contracts for food from other states, will demand that the food be delivered. The supplier states will refuse to deliver what little they have and this could trigger war between states. As the famine becomes more severe, people from cities could attack other cities to confiscate their food. In addition, the government may attempt to confiscate food supplies. The situation will probably build quite rapidly and some people will try to warehouse food supplies due to the emergency before it becomes a famine.

Another scripture sheds some light on this time as well:

> *Behold, vengeance cometh speedily upon the inhabitants of the earth, a day of wrath, a day of burning, a day of desolation, of weeping, of mourning, and of lamentation and as a whirlwind it shall come upon all the face of the earth, saith the Lord. And upon my house shall it begin, and from my house shall it go forth, saith the Lord. First among those among you, saith the Lord, who have professed to know my name and have not known me, and have blasphemed against me in the midst of my house, saith the Lord.* (D&C 112:24-26)

This is obviously referring to the time we are talking about, because the vengeance of which he speaks has not yet started. It comes quickly like a whirlwind and ultimately spreads to all the earth, but it begins "upon my house." When he says "my house" he is not referring to the temple. He is referring to the house of Israel, which consists of Ephraim or the church. He defined the nation of his house as the US in Isaiah 2 discussed above. So the trouble will begin here on the church.

The question now begged is why? What is it about the church that causes the trouble to come upon it? We showed earlier in the discussion of the apostasy of the church that we are pretty much like gentiles with little to distinguish us. Since the beginning of the troubles obviously have to do with food, this must be the factor. If the beginning of the trouble is a shortage of food then it all makes sense.

On a talk show a few weeks ago, a man called in and asked if the government had laws against the storage of emergency food. The host told him that he did not think so and asked, "What about the Mormons? They all have a year's supply of food in their basements." And this, I think, is the problem. The people of this country perceive that we all have a year's supply or more. The fact is that only about three percent have a year's supply and about 30 percent have three month's supply or less. So we are far from the perceived ideal of all having a year's supply. But that does not matter.

In recent months, the church has made a great show of giving surplus food to other countries and to agencies who distribute it. The church has opened use of the canneries to other churches and groups. There is nothing wrong with this but the notoriety sends the message that the Mormons have so much food they cannot use it all and are giving it away by the truck load. The perception is that we have lots of food, not only in our basements, but also in warehouses and canneries. And when the food shortage comes, someone will look toward us and say, "Let's go get that food."

It may be the government who tries to come and get the "surplus" to distribute to other areas. What will happen when 97 percent of the members and most of the gentiles say, "We have no food?" The same thing will happen that happened in Waco with the Branch Davidians. The government claimed that they had illegal weapons inside. For that, they killed 87 helpless and trapped men, women including 17 little children. When it was over, they found no illegal weapons, but only ones legally bought. The surviving members were tried on entirely different charges and sent to prison.

So when the people start protesting that they have no food, will the government start breaking into and raiding homes? It is very likely since that is the pattern of federal enforcement agencies of late. I believe, though, that the more likely scenario is that the government will demand the food from the brethren thinking that they will not only turn over any surplus the general church has, but also will "command" the members to turn over their own supplies. They may begin to rough up the presidency and other general authorities; maybe arrest them. This may cause the faithful to rise up and attack the federal agents who are doing it. This is something that would happen very quickly in a matter of a day or two. Those who do have their year's supply are very adamant about protecting it and most have the means, so it will not be an easy task. In fact, it will not happen. Many attackers may lose their lives as well as many members living here.

As soon as this battle is over, the food shortage will be extremely bad and people will begin to war with one another both in mobs and individually killing for food. There will be no work and chaos will reign in this land. The entire fabric of government will break down and anarchy will exist. There will be famine in the US accompanied by marauding mobs. All of these things have been foretold in other places and most are familiar with these prophecies. Those things will happen at this time. The terrible trouble will begin in the US and the country, as a nation, will be destroyed.

The famine will be felt in other nations as well. Russia has announced that it has a serious shortfall in its wheat crop again this year as it has for the past several years. Russia plans to purchase some 30 million tons. The question is, if there is a serious shortage in the US, where will the wheat come from? Perhaps from Canada, but if there is a crop failure in the US, it will affect Canada as well.

When the difficulty begins with the church, coupled with the food shortage around the world, the missionaries will be forced to return home. This will end the taking of the gospel to the gentiles, or the fulfilling of the times of the gentiles. This is a major milestone and marks the end of the preliminary events setting the stage for the tribulation. The stage is now set and the lights are turned down for the first act in the "great and marvelous work and a wonder" that is about to begin. But you thought the marvelous work and a wonder was the restoration of the gospel and growth of the church? Not so! Read on.

Chapter II

Act I The Tribulation of Israel

With the fulfilling of the times of the gentiles, the preliminary signs of the last days were completed and the world was set for the next event or sequence of predefined events. All the prophecies we relate to the restoration of the gospel and taking it into all the world have now been fulfilled. The order of society and of the church have now changed because of the civil war and unrest that has torn the United States apart. The food shortages and resulting warfare have begun and are continuing as this phase of temporal history closes.

At this point, the civil war in the United States will cause political upheaval in all the world. The US has been the great provider and the collapse of this nation will cause great alarm and fear among our allies. The food shortage will affect the entire world. The nations will be in consultation and will seek solutions to the situation. Travel will cease and workers will have no jobs nor income. It is not clear if all workers will be in this situation in the world, but Isaiah, in the scripture quoted above says that, "all who work for wages shall suffer distress." (19:10). There will be great travail and insecurity at this time.

While the people mourn, a great event takes place that changes the course of the world. This event will start the clock running for the final events which are timed and placed in sequence by the prophecies pertaining to this next period called the tribulation. It is called the tribulation because it is the separation of the righteous and wicked, particularly among the Lord's people, or Israel. The Latin word from which it comes means to thresh. In the modern sense, tribulation is suffering or affliction. The Lord has referred to this as the crucible of affliction. His people are afflicted to cause them to repent of their sins and idolatry. We mentioned above that this is done is by allowing the people to be taken captive. This has always been the pattern. It will be no different this time as we shall see. Returning to Isaiah 19:

Egypt's spirit shall be drained from within; I will frustrate their plans, and they will resort to the idols and to spiritists, to mediums and witchcraft. Then will I deliver the Egyptians into the hand of a cruel master; a harsh ruler will subject them, says my Lord, the Lord of Hosts. (Isaiah 19:3-4)

This is part of the same reference cited in the previous chapter. The civil wars and anarchy will bring the United States to its knees and sap its spirit and strength. At that time, the country will be invaded by a tyrant, which Isaiah calls the archtyrant or King of Assyria, as we shall later see.

Many have supposed that this nation would endure forever and that no nation would ever be able to invade and/or conquer us. This is pure arrogance. The ancient Egyptians believed the same thing. They were the first great civilization but they were finally conquered by the Greeks and then the Romans, including others who invaded their outer lands. The Assyrians became the most powerful followed by the Babylonians. The Persians conquered the Babylonians but were easily defeated by the Greeks who were conquered by the Romans. The great Roman Empire finally fell at the hands of people they called barbarians. So to believe that we cannot be conquered, or that there is some divine protection over us, is more than arrogance, it is ignorance of the prophecies concerning this land.

The opening scene in what I call Act One of the last days drama, is the rise of a great world ruler whose ascent will be most rapid. It will be precipitated by the worsening world condition and many will look for a temporal savior. This was the case in Germany during the great depression. The people looked for someone to give them jobs. Hitler did so. He also caused the death of millions of his people and the destruction of his country. The people will look for someone to restore order and save the world.

The Book of Isaiah is filled with details about this person, as are the Revelation of John and the Book of Daniel. We will look at these prophecies. At the front of the book is a Last Days Chart. This chart puts in chronological sequence the events of the last days. Refer to this chart as we proceed through the chapters of this book. The beginning of Act One, or this chapter, is point 0 which is the left edge of the chart. Notice that the chart goes from

0 to a little past 7. These are years and represent the two periods of 42 months of literal time of the last days. They are the last 42 months of the sixth seal and the first 42 months of the seventh seal. This is when all the events prophesied for these times will occur. Since we know that the seals represent defined blocks of time, we can tell with pretty good accuracy when this all takes place.

If the Lord operated according to our calendars, the sixth seal should be closed when the century ends on December 31, 2000. (Most people erroneously think the new millennium begins on January 1, 2000.) The last 42 months of the sixth seal would then have had to begin on July 1, 1997. The seventh seal would then begin on January 1, 2001, the first year of the new millennium. Of course we have passed July 1, 1997 by a couple of years but the fact that we are near the end of the sixth seal is obvious. There are those who maintain that the coming of the Savior must be out about 2030 or some other far off time because of the work still remaining as they suppose. Our calendars cannot be off more than a few years. The variable here is that the Lord has his time table and is not bound by our calendar. But we can be assured the time is near and we should not be lulled into a sense of false security.

The Rise of the King of Assyria

Whenever the precise date is, we will know exactly when the clock begins to run and it begins to run with the occurrence of two significant events. The first event is the rise of the King of Assyria. We will first look at the description of him in Revelation then examine the details that Isaiah gives, which are quite revealing and complete:

> *And I stood upon the sand of the sea, and saw a beast rise up out of the sea, having seven heads and ten horns, and upon his heads the name of blasphemy. And the beast which I saw was like unto a leopard, and his feet were as the feet of a bear, and his mouth as the mouth of a lion: and the dragon gave him his power, and his seat, and great authority. And I saw one of his heads as it were wounded to death; and his deadly wound was healed: and all the world wondered after the beast. And they worshipped the dragon which gave power unto the beast: and*

they worshipped the beast, saying, Who is like unto the beast? who is able to make war with him? And there was given unto him a mouth speaking great things and blasphemies; and power was given him to continue forty and two months. And he opened his mouth in blasphemy against God, to blaspheme his name, and his tabernacle, and them that dwell in heaven. And it was given unto him to make war with the saints, and to overcome them: and power was given him over all kindreds, and tongues, and nations. And all that dwell upon the earth shall worship him, whose names are not written in the book of life of the Lamb slain from the foundation of the world. (Rev. 13:1-8)

This stunning vision which John saw has piqued the imagination of every student of Revelation and there has been much diverse opinion about it. The majority of non-LDS Bible commentators believe this refers to the Roman Empire at the time of John and that the beast or antichrist was Nero. Other opinions hold differing ideas. Some believe that the vision is of the latter days. Most LDS commentators, however, believe it to be the latter-day rise to power of a powerful kingdom and ruler. These verses tell us several things by which we can determine much about the beast. First John says the beast is like a leopard with the mouth of a lion and feet of a bear. Animals represent nations and kingdoms and this description is no different. Daniel gives some additional information on the beast:

And four great beasts came up from the sea, diverse one from another. The first was like a lion, and had eagle's wings: I beheld till the wings thereof were plucked, and it was lifted up from the earth, and made stand upon the feet as a man, and a man's heart was given to it. And behold another beast, a second, like to a bear, and it raised up itself on one side, and it had three ribs in the mouth of it between the teeth of it: and they said thus unto it, Arise, devour much flesh. After this I beheld, and lo another, like a leopard, which had upon the back of it four wings of a fowl; the beast had also four heads; and dominion was given to it. After this I saw in the night visions, and behold a fourth beast, dreadful and terrible, and strong exceedingly; and it had great iron teeth: it devoured and brake in pieces, and stamped the residue with the feet of it: and it was diverse from all the beasts that were before it; and it had ten horns. I considered the horns, and, behold, there came up among them another little horn, before whom there were three of the first horns plucked up by the roots: and, behold, in this horn were eyes like the eyes of a man, and a mouth speaking great things...I beheld, and the same horn made war with the saints, and prevailed against them...Thus he said, The fourth beast shall be the fourth kingdom upon the earth, which shall be diverse from all kingdoms, and shall devour the whole earth, and shall tread it down, and break it in pieces. And the ten horns out of this kingdom are ten kings that shall rise: and another shall rise after them; and he shall be diverse from the first, and he shall subdue three kings. And he shall speak great words against the most High, and shall wear out the saints of the most High, and think to change times and laws: and they shall be given into his hand until a time and times and the dividing of time. (Daniel 7:3-8, 21, 23-25)

It is evident that John and Daniel are seeing the same beast although Daniel sees three individual beasts first. The fourth beast is composed of these three beasts as John reports. The first task is to identify the beasts. The first beast Daniel saw was like a lion and had eagle's wings. The lion represents England. The eagle wings represent mobility in prophetic language. England was one of the earliest countries to send its ships around the world and to establish colonies everywhere. It was said that the sun never set on the British Empire. It was a conqueror and colonizer which devoured nations like a lion. Later, Daniel says, the wings were plucked and it was made to stand on its feet as a man and it was given a man's heart. Between World Wars I and II, this colonial expansion stopped and after World War I, the great British fleet was demobilized. The trend then became to free the colonies which proceeded over the next few decades. The image of the man with a man's heart represents this new thinking about the freedom of the rest of mankind.

The bear is a well-known symbol and is applied only to the Soviet Union and now to Russia. The bear is seen lying on its side and when it turns, it has three ribs in its teeth. This beast is a devourer as Russia has always been. Following World War II, the Soviets remained as conquerors in all the lands they supposedly liberated from the Nazis. All of Eastern Europe, Lithuania, Latvia, Estonia and Finland were occupied. Finland was later freed. This nation devoured half of Europe and could not be dislodged. The three ribs represent both the fact that he is a devourer and the three kings he plucks up by the roots. The voice of an angel, presumably, tells the bear to "arise" and "devour much flesh."

The third beast has given people a little more trouble but he gives us enough to identify this creature. The leopard has four heads and the wings of fowl, which means chickens or other domesticated birds. It does not have eagle's wings like the lion. The wings still mean mobility but not as wide-ranging as the lion. Chickens are able to fly over the fence into their neighbor's yards and cause some trouble. In addition, the beast has four heads. Heads are kingdoms or reigns. This is the key.

Germany has been an aggressor for two great wars this century. They have invaded their neighbors and caused a great deal of trouble. The Leopard is a predator too. The four heads serve to identify it by the types of rule they have had. From the time that the country became a nation, it was a monarchy which lasted until the fall of Kaiser Wilhelm II after World War I. Following that they formed the Weimar Republic which lasted for a time until about 1932 when Hitler was made Vice Chancellor. Eventually he and his national socialists took over and ruled to 1945. Since that time it has been a democratic republic. These four governments are the four heads.

So we see that the fourth beast is made up of England, Germany and Russia as the main beasts or components. This is incredible because these nations have been enemies throughout this century. But this "diverse" nation will be different from any of them individually and will have an entirely different character. It is interesting that England and Germany are the two leaders of the present European Union.

Another feature both John and Daniel mention are the 10 horns. These are the same as the 10 toes of Nebuchadnezzar's dream image. They are the kingdoms or nations which are the remnant of the Roman Empire. These are the nations of Europe.

John was told by the angel that these kingdoms did not exist in his day but would exist later, so we know the beast does not pertain to John's time and is not the Roman Empire nor is the antichrist Nero. These are the countries that exist today and a little horn comes up among them. This little horn is the "mouth" of the beast and is the King of Assyria from Isaiah. Assyria in that book is a metaphor for Russia, hence, the little horn is the leader of Russia and the leader of the new giant government which is formed and called the beast. This leader, the Russian president or head, destroys three of the other kings. This does not mean that he destroys the countries but that he removes their leaders. Further, we know the little horn is the one who plucks up these three governments and in Daniel's vision, the bear is seen with the three ribs in his mouth which identifies the bear or Russia with the little horn or king of the great nation now formed.

For some time NATO has been inviting the former Warsaw Pact nations to join the organization. Some have applied for membership. They have asked Russia to join on an advisory basis but Russia, so far, has refused. The little horn is given a mouth and with it he is going to amaze and convince the other nations to follow him and give him their power. John tells us that the ten kings give their power to the beast for a time and they join in a great Eurasian union headed by Russia, England and Germany.

The beast also has seven heads and the names of blasphemy are written on them. Who are the seven heads? This is the clue that has convinced most commentators that it refers to Rome since Rome is built on seven hills. But as was explained earlier, hills and mountains are metaphors for nations or countries. So the seven heads are seven countries but which ones? John gives a hint, or rather, the answer.

John says that one of the heads was wounded to death and was later healed and the world wondered after the beast. It is obvious that if this is to be a Eurasian union, then the countries between Russia and Western Europe will have to be involved. The seven heads are, in fact these six nations who, with the Soviet Union, made up the Warsaw Pact. The head that is wounded is the Soviet Union. In 1990 and 1991 the Soviet Union apparently broke down into 15 republics and the Warsaw Pact was dissolved. This was the "death" of communism the world was told. This was the wound that supposedly killed one of the seven heads.

In the last Russian elections, the communist leaders ran very strong campaigns and were even thought possible winners in the elections. Yeltsin was reelected, however. The main message of the front running communist candidate was that the USSR would have to be reestablished. The reestablishment of the USSR would heal the wounded head of the beast which John reported and the world would be amazed. Two other candidates have said the same thing. Vladimir Zhirinovsky has said exactly the same thing and he was the most popular candidate a couple of years previous when his party won the most votes in the parliamentary elections. Mikhail Gorbachev was also running and he has also stated that the old Soviet Union must be reestablished. There is little doubt that such will eventually happen. Many feel that Boris Yeltsin has merely been a caretaker president while the Russians were carrying out their grand deception. At any rate we will soon see this head healed and the world will be shocked.

John says that the people will worship the beast and will marvel at how powerful he is. Who is able to make war with the beast? This tells us that the beast will have great military might. He will be allied with the Chinese who have millions of men they can marshal for war at once. It is estimated that China can mobilize an army of 100 million men. There has never been an army near this size. John says the beast has the feet of a bear. The feet are the ability to travel and Russia has great mechanized forces, planes and ships to transport large numbers of solders. And he will most certainly use them.

John says the beast was given power over "all kindreds, and tongues, and nations." He will conquer the entire world, a feat no other conqueror has ever done though they have all dreamed of it. John says further that he was given power to make war with the saints and to overcome them. Daniel says that he made war with the saints and prevailed against them and that he wears out the saints. He also says that he, the beast, shall devour the whole earth, and shall tread it down. There are many in the church who expect that the tribulation will pass them by somehow and while the wicked are destroyed or suffer greatly, the saints will be spared. But as we mentioned before, the price of idolatry is captivity and so the saints will be taken captive and this is the harsh ruler and cruel master of Isaiah 19 quoted above. He will not only take captive the Egyptians (Americans) but the members of the church wherever they are. He will take all nations of the world captive.

Both of these prophets give us an important time check in the two accounts. John says the beast is given power 42 months. Daniel says he has power for a time, times and the dividing of times and since this is the same period that John describes as 42 months, it also means three-and-a-half years. Time equals a year, times is two years and the dividing of time is a half year. This same statement is used elsewhere and it means the same in each case. But the beast's reign of terror will last only 42 months. This will take us to the center of the last days chart which is three and a half years. This period is the last 42 months of the sixth seal as we shall see later.

This super state will be the richest and most powerful the world has ever seen. It will combine the military might of Russia, which exceeds any in the world, including the US, with the wealth of the European Union.

The US has high technology weapons systems but the Russians also have very high technology, which we have been sharing with them since the supposed fall of communism. In addition, they have far superior numbers of missiles, planes, ships and men in the armed services. We know that the Chinese will also be allied with him and they bring a potential of 100 million men or more.

> *And with the arms of a flood shall they be overflown from before him, and shall be broken; yea, also the prince of the covenant. And after the league made with him he shall work deceitfully: for he shall come up, and shall become strong with a small people.* (Dan 11:22-23)

One might think the "small people" means a small population but it is speaking of a people who are small, as the Chinese and most Orientals tend to be. They are very numerous and will provide the manpower for the world conquest by the king of Assyria.

The U.S. is actually bankrupt and so far in debt that our national debt is the major issue in all recent national elections. We are on the brink of total economic collapse and when the civil war comes, it will virtually put an end to the government's income. That is when we will be super vulnerable, and we will be delivered into the hand of a cruel master and harsh ruler (Isaiah 19:4).

This great ruler will be an enemy of God and of the Savior and this is why he is called the antichrist. He will hate the righteous Christian people, especially members of the church. He will blaspheme everything holy and eventually people will worship him. John goes on to tell of a second beast or powerful individual who will arise at about this time:

> *And I beheld another beast coming up out of the earth; and he had two horns like a lamb, and he spake as a dragon. And he exerciseth all the power of the first beast before him, and causeth the earth and them which dwell therein to worship the first beast, whose deadly wound was healed. And he doeth great wonders, so that he maketh fire come down from heaven on the earth in the sight of men. And deceiveth them that dwell on the earth by the means of those miracles which he had power to do in the sight of the beast; saying to them that dwell on the earth, that they should make an image to the beast, which had the wound by a sword, and did live. And he had power to give life unto the image of the beast, that the image of the beast should both speak, and cause that as many as would not worship the image of the beast should be killed. And he caused all, both small and great, rich and poor, free and bond, to receive a mark in their right hand, or in their foreheads: And that no man might buy or sell, save he that had the mark, or the name of the beast, or the number of his name. Here is wisdom. Let him that hath understanding count the number of the beast: for it is the number of a man; and his number is Six hundred threescore and six.* (Rev 13:11-18).

Again there is very much information in a few words. We will not only have to deal with the first beast who is the super nation/conqueror but we will have to contend with a second person who will be part of the kingdom of the first beast but will have his own power and dominion within that rule. Some have suggested that the second beast is a successor kingdom to the first super state. But they are contemporaries because they are both taken and cast into the pit. One is called the beast and the other the false prophet:

> *And the beast was taken, and with him the false prophet that wrought miracles before him, with which he deceived them that had received the mark of the beast, and them that worshipped his image. These both were cast alive into a lake of fire burning with brimstone.* (Rev 19:20)

It is clear from this verse that the false prophet, who is clearly the second beast of chapter 13, is contemporary with the first beast and is the one who made the people worship the first beast. The important thing here is to identify the second beast or false prophet.

Duane Crowther in his book *Prophecy—Key to the Future* lists the many ideas people have had over the years about the mark of the beast or the number 666. John makes it clear that it is the number of the name of a man and he challenges anyone of wisdom to "count the number of the beast." I will return to this below but there are other metaphorical clues that are given.

The beast is described as having two horns of a lamb but speaks with the voice of the dragon. The lamb is a well-known symbol of the Savior and so John is telling us that the person is not only a religious figure but a Christian figure or leader. The two horns mean that the man, or his kingdom, has two areas or rule. The kingdom that immediately comes to mind is the only Christian religion or kingdom that has two areas of rule; the Roman Catholic Church.

Throughout the centuries since becoming the official religion in the Roman Empire, the Roman church has had two power roles: ecclesiastical power and temporal power with the pope often serving as the Roman emperor. Even today, the Vatican has diplomatic relations with most countries through papal ambassadors and legates. These offices deal with the various governments as a secular government. In the middle ages when the Roman Church had great temporal power, the pope exercised the power of the state and, although he was not the political ruler, he had power to make people join the official worship of Rome, or worship the "beast" at that time. He and the ecclesiastical courts had power to force people on pain of death to worship the beast. Thousands were martyred in this way and the pope even waged war against different groups he considered heretics. This description seems to exactly fit the person of the pope.

Some time ago, someone figured out that the name the pope wore on his cap worked out to be 666 when the Roman numeral equivalents were added. The members of the church gradually deserted this idea over the years, but this still fits the conditions at the time and whether or not 666 really identifies him, the other evidences surely do. This new beast will do the same things the former popes did. He will force the people to worship the new beast and will order the deaths of all who do not. To fail to worship the head of the super state, the leader of Russia and the world, will cause the heretic to be killed.

A fascinating book was published in 1990 called *The Keys of This Blood* by Malachi Martin, a former Jesuit and currently professor at the Vatican's Pontifical Biblical Institute. He is a Vatican insider and knowledgeable about these matters. The subtitle of the book is *The Struggle for World Dominion Between Pope John Paul II, Mikhail Gorbachev and the Capitalist West.* This book is a very detailed exposition of the views and aspirations of the current pope, John Paul II and the unchanged views of the Catholic Church relative to divine right to rule over mankind.

The pope sees three major players as potential leaders in the coming global government: Mikhail Gorbachev (or his successor), a western leader yet to emerge or be defined, and himself. That he is a major competitor in this struggle for dominion is relatively unperceived by most in the world, but this book lays bare his desire and plans to emerge as the world ruler in the sense of the ancient Holy Roman Pope/Emperors. The first part of the book summarizes who the players are and the aims of each. The rest of the book is a detailed coverage of the Pope's efforts and policies to carry out his ambitions. Here are a few quotes from the first part:

> *An isolated figure Karol Wojtyla may have been in the fall of 1976—at least for many Westerners. But two years later, in October of 1978, when he emerged from the Sistine Chapel in Rome as Pope John Paul II, the 264th successor to Peter the Apostle, he was himself the head of the most extensive and deeply experienced of the three global powers that would, within a short time, set about ending the nation system of world politics that has defined*

> *human society for over a thousand years.*
> *It is not too much to say, in fact, that the chosen purpose of John Paul's pontificate—the engine that drives his papal grand policy and that determines his day-to-day, year-by-year strategies—is to be the victor in that competition, now well under way.* (p. 17)
> *There exist on this earth,...only three Internationales. The Golden Internationale was his shorthand term for the financial powers of the world—the Transnationalist and Internationalist globalist leaders of the West.*
> *The Red Internationale was, of course, the Leninist-Marxist Party-State of the Soviet Union,...*
> *The third geopolitical contender—The Roman Catholic Church; the Black Internationale—was destined...to be the ultimate victor in any contention with those rivals.* (p. 21)

After the pope's visit to Poland shortly after his election, comments on his speech were published revealing his message:

> *A new factor has been added to the presently accepted formula of international contention. It is a Slavic Pope. The imbalance in our thinking has been unobtrusively but decisively and, as it were, overnight corrected by the emergence of John Paul. For his persona has refocused international attention away from the two extremes, East and West, and on the actual center of change, Mittel-europa, the central bloc of Europe's nations.* (p. 22)
> *In John Paul's geopolitical analysis, Europe from the Atlantic to the Urals is a giant seesaw of power. Europe from the Baltic to the Adriatic Sea is the center of that power. The Holy Father's battle was to control that center.*
> *World commentary and opinion aside, therefore, the point of John Paul's foray into Poland was not merely that he was a religious leader. The point was that he was more. He was geopolitical pope. He was a Slav who had come from a nation that had always viewed its own role and its fate within a geopolitical framework—within the large picture of world forces. Now he had served notice that he intended to take up and effectively exercise once more the international role that had been central to the tradition of*

Rome, and to the very mandate Catholics maintain was conferred by Christ upon Peter and upon each of his successors. (p. 22)

It was the first distinguishing mark of John Paul's career as Pontiff that he had thrown off the straitjacket of papal inactivity in major world affairs. On his trip to Poland in 1979,...he signaled the opening of the millennium endgame. He became the first of the three players to enter the new geopolitical arena.

...it was not to be wondered that suddenly, and without any of the laborious worldwide politicking that normally attends such matters, Karol Wojtyla was placed at the head of the world's only existing and fully operating georeligious institution: the universal organization of his Roman Catholic Church.

Though in one sense his new life as Roman Pontiff was a very public one, another dimension of that life gave John Paul a certain invaluable immunity from suspicious and prying eyes. That white robe and skullcap, that Fisherman's Ring on his index finger, the panoply of papal liturgy, the appanage of pontifical life, all meant that the rank and file of world leaders, as well as most observers and commentators, would see him almost exclusively as a religious leader. (p. 23)

A second advantage for Pope John Paul in the peculiar papal immunity he enjoyed was that the champions he expected to enter the endgame arena did not expect him to be a contender. They failed to read him in the same geopolitical terms he applied to them. He was not seen as a threat even in those political, cultural and financial circles outside the Roman Church where there has always been an abiding fear of "caesaro-papism." A fear that implied an ugly suspicion of totalitarian and antidemocratic ambition in any pope, whoever he might be. The ancient but still entertained fear that if any Roman pope had his way, he would damage or abolish democratic freedoms—above all, the freedom to think, to experiment and to develop politically. There seemed to be no fear of John Paul as a potential Caesar. (pp. 24-25)

> *Despite this cyclone of questions and lethal arguments that swirled around himself and his papacy, however, this young and stubborn Pope John Paul II remained the steady-as-you-go Vicar of Christ for whom everything—no matter how important it might appear to others—was and would remain secondary to his central perspective and preoccupation: the progress and outcome of the international, winner-take-all competition.* (p. 91)

In the years since the publication of this book, the pope has continued his rhetoric in favor of the new world order. He has slightly altered his viewpoint from that presented above. Since 1990, Gorbachev has been removed as head of the Soviet Union and of Russia but his esteem has grown and he has truly become the darling of the western world and *Time's* man of the decade. He ran for election as the president of Russia. Although he was far behind in the popularity polls, he is popular with the KGB and the Russian Army who hold the reins of power there. If they want him back in power, he will eventually return whether he is popular with the people or not.

The pope has since made many statements about Gorbachev stating that he is the one who can unite the East and West in the great superstate from the "Atlantic to the Urals." These statements show the real likelihood of these two men forming the leadership of the super global government which is foreseen by all who are aware of current political trends and which was predicted by John. These two men, or their successors, are the likely humans who are the two beasts of Revelation 13. And, as was made clear in that chapter and in the book cited, the aim is a complete end to all nations and the formation of a global nation with these men at the head.

Reading the book, we get the feeling that the pope is a benign and loving man who cares deeply for humanity. The same image is broadcast about Gorbachev, but we must remember that he (Gorbachev) is the architect of the slaughter in Afghanistan and of countless others during his rule. We have ample historical record of the abuses of the Catholic Church during its reign of terror over the centuries also. The history of the cruelties of these two regimes is painted accurately by John in his descriptions of these beasts. When they come to power, as they surely will, they will be "harsh rulers and cruel masters" as they subdue mankind through the power of their real master; the dragon. Isaiah does not mention the false prophet or the second beast, but he has much to say about the first beast whom he calls the king of Assyria.

> *Therefore the anger of the Lord is kindled against his people: he draws back his hand against them and strikes them;...He raises an ensign to distant nations and summons them from beyond the horizon. Forthwith they come, swiftly and speedily. Not one of them grows weary, nor does any stumble; they do not drowse or fall asleep. Their waist-belts come not loose nor their sandal thongs undone. Their arrows are sharp; all their bows are strung. The tread of their war-horses resembles flint; their chariot wheels revolve like a whirlwind. They have the roar of a lion; they are aroused like young lions: growling, they seize the prey, and escape, and none comes to the rescue. He shall be stirred up against them in that day, even as the Sea is stirred up. And should one look to the land, there too shall be a distressing gloom, for the daylight shall be darkened by an overhanging mist.* (Isaiah 5:26-30)

Isaiah describes the invaders in these verses who are shown to be a well disciplined army. They come from beyond the horizon or far from here. The Lord raises an ensign, which is a signal flag used on ships and in this case it is a signal for the tyrant to come. The description here gives us a picture of a mighty, irresistible and mechanized army and there is no help when it comes. There are no allies to call on because the European nations we have aided will be giving their power and strength to this beast. He, the tyrant, is stirred up against Israel or the church. The entire land will be gloomy and covered with smoke and the darkness of war.

> *Woe to the garlands of glory of the drunkards of Ephraim! Their crowning splendor has become as fading wreaths on the heads of the opulent overcome with wine. My Lord has in store one mighty and strong: as a ravaging hailstorm sweeping down, or like an inundating deluge of mighty waters, he will hurl them to the ground by his hand. The proud garlands of the drunkards of Ephraim shall be trodden underfoot. And the fading wreaths, the crowns of*

glory on the heads of the opulent, shall be like the first-ripe fruit before summer harvest: he who sees it devours it the moment he has hold of it. Therefore, by incomprehensible speech and a strange tongue must he speak to these people. (Isaiah 28:1-4, 11)

The Lord explains that the invasion comes as a result of the apostasy (the fading wreaths) of Ephraim or the church. He characterizes us as drunk with wine. This is a metaphor for idolatry. We are drunk with the wine of Babylon; the desire for things and this has made us insensible to the things we should be thinking and doing which is preparing Zion for the coming of the Savior.

Instead the Lord has prepared a mighty and strong one whom he compares to a ravaging hailstorm and as deluge of waters. Hand is a metaphor for a servant of the Lord who can either be a good or bad servant; a blessing or a scourge. In this case his hand is the king of Assyria who will hurl the drunkards of Ephraim to the ground. The garlands of glory, the leaders and heroes including the sports heroes, will be trodden underfoot. Remember in John's vision of the beast, he had the feet of a bear and stamped many people. This is part of that action.

The Lord also explains in these verses not quoted above, that the people will not listen to his counsel because we are caught up in Babylon. In verse 11, quoted above, he says that he must therefore speak to us in a different language. There is a double meaning here. The strange and incomprehensible tongue is described elsewhere also:

...Where are those who levied the tax? Where are the ones who appraised the towers? The insolent people are not to be seen, a nation of incomprehensible speech, whose babbling tongue was unintelligible. (Isaiah 33:18-19)

When the invasion is over and Ephraim is rescued, Isaiah asks where are they and describes the invaders as a nation of incomprehensible and unintelligible speech. This same speech is described in another scripture as tinkling speech. It is obviously Chinese that he refers to. Daniel refers to them also:

And after the league made with him he shall work deceitfully: for he shall come up, and shall become strong with a small people. (Daniel 11:23)

The small people are not few in number as many have supposed but rather they are a physically small people but very numerous. The Chinese will be allies of Russia and make up much of the army of the beast. These will be our invaders and they will be harsh and cruel as we have see in their invasions of Tibet, Burma and elsewhere. The Lord goes on:

> *O you deaf, listen; O you blind, look and see! Who is blind but my own servant, or so deaf as the messenger I have sent? Who is blind like those I have commissioned, as uncomprehending as the servant of the Lord seeing much but not giving heed, with open ears hearing nothing? It is the will of the Lord, that, because of his righteousness they magnify the law and become illustrious. Instead, they are a people plundered and sacked, all of them trapped in holes, hidden away in dungeons. They have become a prey, yet no one rescues them, a spoil, yet none demands restitution. Who among you hearing this will take heed of it hereafter, and be mindful and obey? Who is it that hands Jacob over to plunder and Israel to despoilers, if not the Lord, against whom we have sinned? For they have no desire to walk in his ways or obey his law. So in the heat of his anger he pours out on them the violence of war, till it envelops them in flames—yet they remain unaware—till it sets them on fire; yet they take it not to heart.* (Isaiah 42:22-25)

The Lord, through Isaiah, is speaking to the church and telling us that we are blind and deaf because we are caught up in idolatry. We are blind because we see what is happening both in the church and in the world but we do not comprehend what we see. We are seeing the collapse of the US Constitution but people go on as usual pursuing their idols. He hints here that his servant whom he has commissioned is more blind than others. With our ears open, we hear nothing. The idea is "all is well in Zion."

The Lord's desire is that we obey his precepts and law thereby becoming illustrious, which is a code word for translated. His righteousness is an important metaphor also which will be discussed in the next section. But instead of realizing this glorious blessing, we are taken captive, sacked and plundered with many thrown into dungeons and others in hiding or fleeing into the country. There is no one to immediately rescue them (us).

He admonishes us to return to reality and listen and obey because it is the Lord who is causing the captivity and oppression for this very purpose. Captivity has always been the means of purging the Lord's people of their idolatry. A powerful captor has to come and strip the people of all their idols. Then and only then, will the people begin to repent and return to the Lord for a while. The final verse shows our blindness because we will not change until the very flames of war envelop us.

Because this beast, the antichrist or archtyrant is of primary importance, or will be, to the church members living during the next few years, it is important to look at a few more of the descriptive prophecies concerning him from the visions of Isaiah.

> *The Lord will bring upon you and your people and your father's house a day unlike any since Ephraim broke away from Judah—the day of the king of Assyria. In that day the Lord will signal for the flies from the far rivers of Egypt and for the bees in the land of Assyria. And they will come and settle with one accord in the riverbeds of the prairie and in rocky ravines, and by all ditches and water holes. In that day my Lord will use a razor hired at the River—the king of Assyria—to shave your head and the hair of your legs, and to cut off even your beard.* (Isaiah 7:17-20)

Isaiah uses metaphor to explain the invasion for those who have learned the manner of prophesying of the Jews. The invasion by the king of Assyria, which he calls "the day of the king of Assyria," will be unlike any invasion in history in its magnitude and terror. Even the name sounds like a Hitchcock title and it inspires horror and dread to read it, if we are not blind and deaf.

The flies and bees are metaphors for warring units, in this case winged units or planes. Water of various kinds is people. Rivers are moving people and usually represent armies. The planes and other fighters will come and settle by all ditches and water holes or settlements and groups of people.

The final metaphor pictures the real horror of the invasion. The king of Assyria, who is here identified as the razor, is the Lord's hired barber. The body being shaved is the church and the hair represents classes of people; the head are the rulers and leaders, the legs the young and the beard represents the elderly. He will have no mercy on any.

> *Woe to those who enact unjust laws, who draft oppressive legislation—denying justice to the needy, depriving the poor of my people of their right, making plunder of widows, mere spoil of the fatherless! What will you do in the day of reckoning when the holocaust overtakes you from afar? To whom will you flee for help? Where will you leave your wealth? There shall nothing remain but to kneel among the captives or fall among the slain. Yet for all this his anger is not abated; his hand is upraised still. Hail the Assyrian, the rod of my anger! He is a staff—my wrath in their hand. I will commission him against a godless nation, appoint him over the people deserving of my vengeance, to pillage for plunder, to spoliate for spoil, to tread underfoot like mud in the streets. Nevertheless, it shall not seem so to him; this shall not be what he has in mind. His purpose shall be to annihilate and to exterminate nations not a few.* (Isaiah 10:1-7)

We discussed the condition of the church today which is precipitating the captivity and one of the major sins of which the Lord condemns us is injustice. We are not taking care of the poor and the fatherless in our midst and for this he says we will kneel among the captives or lie with the slain when the holocaust comes.

Many reports have been produced and studies made showing the state of our culture in Utah. I cannot speak with authority of other states, but this is the only place where church members are in the majority and they hold most offices in the state. Due to this fact, we will not be able to justify our sins with regard to these groups and will kneel among the captives.

The LDS public officials in this state are recognized and given honor including front-row seats in General Conference and much coverage in church publications. These same people in the past few decades have enacted some of the most oppressive legislation in the country. They have burdened us with extremely high taxes and regulations that inhibit the exercise of our agency. RDAs have been set up to confiscate private property at the whim of these modern King Noah's in the name of urban improvement. They then sell or give the property to developers to build beautiful new "great and spacious" buildings which then bring more income to government. As Isaiah says, these people are accomplices of robbers and renegades who deprive the people for bribes. They share in the development by taking kickbacks and enriching themselves. For this the Lord condemns them for making spoil of those who are unable to defend themselves.

A recent study published in the *Deseret News* shows the condition of the poor and needy in our state and points out the fact that while taxes and cost of living have risen dramatically in the last few years, wages in Utah have been dropping. ("Utah fails to help poor..."*Deseret News*, 26 Apr 1996). In the meantime the state budget has soared to over $6 billion annually. It has more than tripled in 10 years. In spite of this, we have many families with an adult working provider who cannot earn above a poverty wage. Another article pointed out that Utah is quite unique in the country in the fact that it imposes income taxes upon people living below the official poverty level. At the same time, we spend more than $1 billion on an idolatrous Olympic spectacle which will probably not take place. It does demonstrate where our treasure and our hearts are.

The Lord sends his scourge, the king of Assyria, the "rod of his anger" and commissions him against us. The king of Assyria, however, does not know that this is his purpose. He thinks he is doing it on his own to annihilate people and exterminate nations. In other words, we have an exterminator about to be turned loose on us.

> *Then the Lord said, Just as my servant Isaiah has gone naked and barefoot for three years as a sign and portent against Egypt and Cush, so shall the king of Assyria lead away the captives of Egypt and the exiles of Cush, both young and old, naked and barefoot, with buttocks uncovered—to Egypt's shame. Men shall be appalled and perplexed at Cush, their hope, and at Egypt, their boast. In that day shall the inhabitants of this isle say, See what has become of those we looked up to, on whom we relied for help and deliverance from the king of Assyria. How shall we ourselves escape?* (Isaiah 20:3-6)

This prophecy is against Egypt and Cush which are metaphorical names for the US and Canada. The king of Assyria will take the people of these two countries captive for three and a half years leading them off barefoot and with bare behinds. The captivity comes following the civil war and unrest which weakens the US so that it cannot defend itself.

This is a gruesome picture and since we, Ephraim, live in Egypt, this will be the fate of the members too. The people of other nations in this hemisphere, which is a huge island separated from Eurasia by water, will be dismayed because they looked to the US and Canada for protection. They wonder how they will escape and of course they will not because he is given dominion over all nations, kindreds and peoples, as both John and Daniel told us.

The end condition after this event occurs is the captivity of the world. Of course the beast has his allies such as China and the countries of Europe and we do not know what effect his reign may have on them. If this century is any indication, the nations of Europe will become much like the Warsaw Pact nations who had puppet Soviet governments with the people under their harsh rule and in subjection but under conditions less severe than the other conquered countries, such as our own.

The Rise of the Davidic King

About the same time as the beast rises to power, there will be another person appear on the scene whose life will be of great importance to the righteous. The Lord gave us a statement about him that has caused considerable speculation among writers of books about last-days prophecy. Again, the writers have skipped many scriptures relating to this man and have relied instead on the speculations of speakers of 100 years ago. The Lord said:

> *Behold, I say unto you, the redemption of Zion must needs come by power; Therefore, I will raise up unto my people a man, who shall lead them like as Moses led the children of Israel. For ye are the children of Israel, and out of the seed of Abraham, and ye must needs be let out of bondage by power, and with a stretched out arm.* (D&C 103:15-17)

Some have thought that this person is Joseph Smith who will somehow be reincarnated and return to lead the people to Zion. When he was president, some thought it might be Brigham Young because they assumed that the retaking of Zion, or the land where it will be, would take place soon. It is neither of these men because both are dead and the dead do not return to minister in the flesh. Both Joseph and Brigham finished their ministries and left. They would have to be resurrected and celestial beings cannot dwell on this telestial earth. So we must look elsewhere for the identity of the man. Strangely enough, he has been definitely identified in scripture we have had since the beginning of the restored church.

With the unsealing of Isaiah, we can see the meaning in other scriptures which we have read over and over without beginning to understand. To our amazement we find that this great personage is discussed in many places and in fact, Joseph Smith identified him. What I am going to show you in the following scriptures will be so new to most of you, although thousands of members know these things well, that you may have difficulty shifting gears in your thinking to realize what is really being said. But once you have done so, the light will shine and you will see things you had not dreamed. The events in the rest of this chapter are so new that most members have never heard of them, but they will have a profound affect on your thinking and upon your life for the better. This thinking change should begin with an examination of this great and important man.

> *The people walking in darkness have seen a bright light; on the inhabitants of the land of the shadow of death has the light dawned. Thou has enlarged the nation and increased its joy; they rejoice at thy presence as men rejoice at harvest time, or as men are joyous when they divide spoil. For thou has smashed the yoke that burdened them, the staff of submission, the rod of those who subjected them, as in the day of Midian's defeat. And all boots used in battle and tunics rolled in blood have become fuel for bonfires. For to us a child is born, a son appointed, who will shoulder the burden of government. He will be called Wonderful Counselor, one Mighty in Valor, a Father for Ever, a Prince of Peace—that sovereignty may be extended and peace have no end; that, on the throne of David and over his kingdom, his rule may be established and upheld by justice and righteousness from this time forth and forever. The zeal of the Lord of Hosts will accomplish it.* (Isaiah 9:2-7)

These verses have been quoted often and all who have listened to the wonderful Handel oratorio, The Messiah, will recognize the source for the song, "For Unto Us a Child is Born." Everyone, including nearly all members of the church, has assumed that this is a messianic prophecy looking to the birth of the Savior. The scripture is messianic in a sense because it talks of a deliverer to free the people from bondage, but this is not the Christ.

The message is addressed to the "people walking in darkness." We have again assumed that this was the apostate world among whom the Savior came as a bright light. It is true that he did so. But this book was written for Israel only, not gentiles and was written for those of us living today. Another prophecy of the birth of the Savior is of little value because he has already come and all of us know and many of us have a divine witness of his coming. He is prophesying of a last-days event as all the prophecies in Isaiah are doing. To be sure, Isaiah talks about the Savior in many places, but this is not one of them except that the Savior was and is a type of this great last-days deliverer.

The people walking in darkness refers to the church today. Isaiah explains that because of the idolatry and injustice of the members of the church, he has ceased to speak to them through the designated oracles.

This man will occupy the throne of David over Israel which the Lord did not do. The Savior is now God, the father and the son, and his sitting on the throne of David would be like the governor of Utah becoming the mayor of Loa.

> *Procrastinate, and become bewildered; preoccupy yourselves, until you cry for help. Be drunk, but not with wine; stagger, but not from strong drink. The Lord has poured out on you a spirit of deep sleep: he has shut your eyes, the prophets; he has covered your heads, the seers....But my Lord says, Because these people approach me with the mouth and pay me homage with their lips, while their heart remains far from me—their piety toward me consisting of the commandments of men learned by rote—therefore it is that I shall again astound these people with wonder upon wonder, rendering void the knowledge of their sages, the intelligence of their wise men insignificant.* (Isaiah 29:9-10, 13-14)

Previously he called Ephraim drunkards. He repeats the same

charge saying we are drunk but not from strong drink. We are in the drunken stupor of idolatry and walking in darkness because he has shut our eyes covered our heads who are the prophets and seers. Our worship of him and piety are learned by rote as the commandments of men.

These verses were often quoted by a well-known and loved apostle who applied them to the world outside the church. But the sad truth is, they apply to us. This is very unsettling news, or should be. What he is saying is that he has stopped giving us revelation through the prophets and seers.

I can hear the gasp of alarm as you read this. Can it be possible? It can be and is because the Lord has said it. He is letting us wander in the darkness without revelation as our guide, hence his address to "the people walking in darkness."

Back to the previous scripture (Isaiah 9:2-7) then, the people walking in darkness are the members of the church today who are temporarily cut off from revelation from the Savior. These people are walking in the "land of the shadow of death." This is the United States after the invasion by the beast. It truly becomes a land under the shadow of death and the people are taken into captivity.

The ancient scene of the people of Israel in bondage in ancient Egypt is being reenacted, hence the name of Egypt applied to the United States today. In the midst of this terrible suffering and bondage, a light appears. It is a messiah or savior, but not the Lord. It is the one mighty and strong whom the Lord said would come to take them out of bondage. As stated in D&C 103 cited above, the people of Israel must be led out of bondage by power with a stretched out arm. The Lord never did this personally. But he uses his arm which is a metaphor for a servant and this term is used throughout Isaiah. Isaiah speaks of two arms; one is the beast or king of Assyria who is the Lord's scourge and referred to as an arm and the other is the one mighty and strong, who is his righteous arm who will save the people.

This man then rescues the people from bondage of the beast or king of Assyria. The people rejoice when they see him because he is their deliverer and smashes the yoke of captivity just as Moses did in his day. This is a very powerful identification of the man. He is talking about literal bondage as he uses the example of the defeat of 120,000 Midianites by Gideon and his 300 (Judges 7:19-23). This was a miraculous event and was not accomplished by strength of arms alone. In addition, the clothing and equipment of the invaders will be burned as fuel.

Where people have trouble is with the last couple of verses. When it says "a child is born," the mind immediately sees the babe in the manger. But this son is born not of Mary but is the spiritual offspring of the Lord. This is one of the major metaphors of the scriptures. The Lord is the bridegroom and the church is the wife. The righteous members are the offspring of this union. This child's birth is the same kind of birth and he will come from this union. He is the child in Revelation 12 depicted on the cover and discussed below.

He will sit upon the throne of David and preside over his kingdom and will rule forever. This is what is meant by the "government will be upon his shoulders" in the KJV and he will "shoulder the burden of government" in the Gileadi translation. The Lord never did set up a temporal government with himself as king. His rule was spiritual and although he was the *de jure* king of Israel, he was never crowned and so did not act as the government. This latter-day king will, however, literally sit on the throne of David and will be the temporal ruler of Israel. The kingdom will be reestablished and will never more be given to another. This is what is meant by the kingdom being given to the saints. He will rule by justice and righteousness, which we will see, are two of the names given him.

> *A shoot [rod] will spring up from the stock [stem] of Jesse and a branch from its graft [roots] bear fruit. The Spirit of the Lord will rest upon him—the spirit of wisdom and of understanding, the spirit of counsel and of valor, the spirit of knowledge and of the fear of the Lord. His intuition will be guided by the fear of the Lord; he will not judge by what his eyes see, nor establish proof by what his ears hear. He will judge the poor with righteousness, and with equity arbitrate for the lowly in the land; he will smite the earth with the rod of his mouth and with the breath of his lips slay the wicked. Righteousness will be as a band about his waist, faithfulness a girdle round his loins. In that day the sprig [root] of Jesse, who stands for an ensign to the*

peoples, shall be sought by the nations, and his residence shall be glorious. In that day my Lord will again raise his hand to reclaim the remnant of his people—those who shall be left out of Assyria, Egypt, Pathros, Cush, Elam, Shinar, Hammath, and the islands of the sea. He will raise the ensign to the nations and assemble the exiled of Israel; he will gather the scattered of Judah from the four directions of the earth. (Isaiah 11:1-5, 10-12)

These verses have often been quoted and the virtues here are usually assigned to the Savior. Joseph Smith received a clarification about this scripture:

Who is the stem of Jesse spoken of in the 1st, 2d, 3d, 4th, and 5th verses of the 11th chapter of Isaiah? Verily thus saith the Lord: It is Christ. What is the rod spoken of in the first verse of the 11th chapter of Isaiah, that should come of the Stem of Jesse? Behold, thus saith the Lord: It is a servant in the hands of Christ who is partly a descendant of Jesse as well as of Ephraim, or of the house of Joseph, on whom there is laid much power. What is the root of Jesse spoken of in the 10th verse of the 11th chapter? Behold, thus saith the Lord, it is a descendant of Jesse, as well as of Joseph, unto whom rightly belongs the priesthood, and the keys of the kingdom, for an ensign, and for the gathering of my people in the last days. (D&C 113:1-6)

These two scriptures give us a partial description of this man. The man will be a descendant of Jesse, or of the royal Davidic lineage. He will be a righteous ruler because he will judge the people, hence he is a Davidic king. He will be a prophet because he will rely on the Spirit of the Lord which will rest upon him. He will smite the enemies of the people with the rod, or word of his mouth. Rod is a metaphor for word or words, such as Lehi's iron rod which is defined by him as the word of God. But this also means that he will have the power to command even the elements and they will obey him. This is the fulness of the priesthood; the power of Elijah.

Joseph Smith reveals much more. He tells us that the servant is a descendant of Jesse making him of the royal Davidic line, and he is also partly of Ephraim giving him the right to officiate and function with the keys in this dispensation. Much power is laid on him (the one mighty and strong). In verse 5, Joseph asks who the root is. This is parallelism and the root and rod are one and the same person but the Lord gives some additional information. He has the right to hold the keys of the kingdom. This means he has the right to preside using all the keys held now by the president of the church. When he comes, then, he will preside by right. We will see later by what right.

The final thing the Lord says about this personage is that his principal mission will be to gather the people of Israel in the last days. It is important to remember this, his primary mission, because other scriptures describe this man in terms of his mission.

The Lord also says "last days" rather than in "these days" indicating that he viewed the last days as yet some way off. Joseph stated that the original King David did not receive the fulness of the priesthood, which is the spirit and power of Elijah. He further states that the priesthood "and the throne and kingdom of David is to be taken from him and given to another by the name of David in the last days, raised up out of his lineage." (DHC 6:253). He also recognized that the "last days" was still sometime in the future.

This king will have the power of Elijah, or fulness of the priesthood since, as Isaiah says above, "he will smite the earth with the rod [word] of his mouth..." The Lord also refers to him as his "hand," a common metaphor in Isaiah. He will raise his "hand" to rescue the people. When he first spoke of the one mighty and strong, he said "I will raise up...." The act of raising is the calling and empowering of a servant. He also says his residence shall be glorious. His residence, of course, is New Jerusalem of which we have much description.

Isaiah gives another quick view of this man in a completely metaphorical context:

> *Rejoice not, all you Philistines, now that the rod which struck you is broken. From among the descendants of that snake shall spring up a viper, and his offspring shall be a fiery flying serpent.* (Isaiah 14:29)

One of the common metaphors for the Savior is the snake. The bronze snake raised up by Moses is a symbol of the Savior. In the Kabbalah, the words for messiah and snake have the same numerical value, hence snake is a common metaphor for him. In this verse, the prophet addresses the Philistines. Well, they do not exist today, but as with all names in Isaiah it is a metaphor. Philistines are the enemies of Israel and they have rejoiced in the troubles of Israel. During the tribulation, the enemies of Israel will also be in captivity and suffering by the king of Assyria.

Isaiah tells the Philistines that they need not rejoice now that the rod, the king of Assyria is broken, because they still have one to fear. A viper will spring up from the among the descendants of that snake. The descendants are the legitimate Davidic lineage continued since Christ and he, the viper, is also a snake and savior of the people, although only in the temporal sense although he will embody the covenant.

The Lord adds that his offspring will be a fiery flying serpent. The Lord refers to the righteous sons from the union of Christ with the woman who represents the church, as his offspring. More specifically, it refers to those who have their call and election made sure. The offspring referred to here are the 144,000 who will be sealed and translated. The term "fiery flying serpent" applies to angels and to translated beings. So the Lord is saying to his and our enemies that although the tyrant is dead who made the world suffer, they will now have to contend with another great leader and his followers. By the use of this term, we know that he and the 144,000 are translated beings. The 144,000 are covered later.

> *Therefore, thus says my Lord the Lord: I lay in Zion a stone, a keystone, a precious cornerstone, a sure foundation. They who believe it will not do rashly.* (Isaiah 28:16)

Jeremiah made a related prophecy in his day:

> *Therefore hear, ye nations, and know, O congregation, what is among them. Hear, O earth: behold I will bring evil upon this people, even the fruit of their thoughts, because they have not hearkened unto my words, nor to my law, but rejected it. Therefore thus saith the Lord, Behold, I will lay stumbling blocks before this people, and the fathers and the sons together shall fall upon them; the neighbour and his friend shall perish. Thus saith the LORD, Behold, a people cometh from the north country, and a great nation shall be raised from the sides of the earth. They shall lay hold on bow and spear; they are*

> *cruel, and have no mercy; their voice roareth like the sea; and they ride upon horses, set in array as men for war against thee, O daughter of Zion.* (Jer 6:18-19, 21-23)

Peter paraphrased these two prophecies:

> *Wherefore also it is contained in the scripture, Behold, I lay in Sion a chief corner stone, elect, precious: and he that believeth on him shall not be confounded. Unto you therefore which believe he is precious: but unto them which be disobedient, the stone which the builders disallowed, the same is made the head of the corner, And a stone of stumbling and a rock of offence, even to them which stumble at the word, being disobedient: whereunto also they were appointed.* (1 Pet 2:6-8)

Isaiah again speaks in metaphor, which is why he has been very difficult for people to understand. In this verse Peter says the Lord is going to lay in Zion a precious stone. Those who believe it or him, will be okay. Peter gives us a hint by calling the stone "him."

Stone is a metaphor for a seer. So what Isaiah is telling us is that in the last days, the Lord would place a precious seer in Zion. This is not talking about an office but a specific person. We are often told to obey the living prophet, but as we have already found out, the Lord is not revealing his will to the church today so this seer must be future.

Jeremiah gives some other information. He states that this will happen in a time of apostasy or the period we called the setup period before the tribulation. He says he will place stumbling blocks before the people and many will fall on them. Blocks are also stones but they are other than the seer upon whom people stumble. They are false teachers who deceive the people by saying "all is well in Zion" when we are in dire apostasy and need to repent. For this, the Lord will send a great nation from the North to punish the "Daughter of Zion."

It could be argued that Jeremiah is talking to the people of his time who are awaiting the invasion of Babylon. The counsel could, of course be applied to his time as most scripture of this type can, but there is one thing that reveals that it is speaking of our time. Jeremiah says that a this great nation will arise from the "sides of the earth." We saw earlier that the beast of the last days will be a great nation extending from the Atlantic to the Pacific or literally from the sides of the earth. The Babylonian Empire occupied a relatively small area at the height of its power. So while the same conditions prevailed then, it is addressing us specifically today.

The stone, or seer, is the same Davidic prophet which was described earlier as having the keys of the kingdom and who acts as directed by the Spirit. Those who accept and follow him, will be able to survive. He will also be a stumbling block to many as Peter said. He will be an offense and many people will not accept him. A prolific, late apostle said that the idea of a Davidic prophet in the last days is heresy and this has pretty much become the official position of the church and a major stumbling block in the last days. When he appears, those who have followed this error, will be offended because he is not of the hierarchy they know, or he did not come to his office in the right way, as they perceive. This will be a very dangerous time. That is one purpose for this book. We must be familiar with who this great and mighty seer is to be, and the actuality of his coming. He has been foretold by Isaiah, John, Joseph Smith and even by the Lord in the Book of Mormon, yet there are those who deny that he will come. He is the forerunner of Christ, the very Elias as Joseph said (D&C 113) and to deny that Elias will come is to deny that the Savior will come. There are many more scriptures dealing with this great individual. One such scripture which signals his role as Elias is also found in Isaiah:

> *A voice calls out, In the desert prepare the way for the Lord; in the wilderness pave a straight highway for our God: every ravine must be raised up, every mountain and hill made low; the uneven ground must become level and rough terrain a plain. For the glory of the Lord shall be revealed and all flesh see it at once. By his mouth the Lord has spoken it. See, my Lord the Lord comes with power; his arm presides for him. His reward is with him; his work precedes him.* (Isaiah 40:3-5, 10)

This has always been considered a messianic prophecy, or prophecy of the coming of the Savior in the meridian of time. Handel created another beautiful solo based on these verses. This is not correct again and an examination will show that it is a last-days event. The important thing here is the "voice" who is calling out. This is the forerunner of the Lord announcing his coming. This has also been most often misquoted since the KJV version is in error. The correct translation is above. The voice calling out is not in the desert but rather is calling to prepare the way for the Lord in the desert. The parallelism shows this: prepare the way in the desert and pave a highway in the wilderness. This will become clear in the next section when we discuss the third of the major events of the last days.

A couple of important metaphors common in Isaiah are used here; mouth and voice. These are the same person. He is Elias, or the forerunner of the second coming just as John the Baptist was in the first. This prophecy is of the second coming, however.

In verse 10, Isaiah says the Lord comes with power, which is the second coming not the first, and "his arm presides for him." Arm is another important metaphor for the Davidic prophet as we discovered in D&C 113. He has the keys and presides by right, hence this scripture is talking about the same person. We will look at this calling of Elias later on as we examine the Book of Revelation and see that he is identified. In the meantime, there are other references to him in Isaiah:

> *Who has raised up Righteousness from the east, calling him to the place of his foot?...I have raised up one from the north who calls on my name, who shall come from the direction of sunrise. He shall come upon dignitaries as on mud, tread them as clay like a potter. Who announced this beforehand, so we would know, declared it ahead of time, that we might say, He was right? Indeed, not one could foretell it, not one make it known; no one has heard from you any prophetic utterance. But to Zion, he shall be her harbinger. I will appoint him as a herald of tidings to Jerusalem.* (Isaiah 41:2, 25-27)

Righteousness is a name for the Davidic king. Another name for New Jerusalem is the City of Righteousness which is the same as the City of David, because that is what it means. The Lord raises up the Davidic king from the east, meaning the middle east. He will also come from the north. He is a Jew after all and therefore comes from the land that is today incorrectly called Israel. He is called from there to this land, the promised land, which is the place of his foot. He originates in the middle east but he is also in the north as well.

In the context of these chapters the Lord is holding a trial and asking for any accusers, the idolaters, to come forward. He mocks the pseudo wise. In verse 26 he continues the mocking tone and asks who was able to foretell these events, namely the coming of the Davidic prophet. No one but God can make these things known. Idols say nothing. The idolaters in Zion cannot predict anything and instead of looking for the signs of his coming, they are spending millions on and planning for the 2002 Olympics.

This prophet and king will be a harbinger or herald. In other words, he will be a prophet to tell us of things to come, especially the second coming. He will also reveal hidden things.

John saw the coming of this great being:

> *And I saw another angel ascending from the east, having the seal of the living God: and he cried with a loud voice to the four angels, to whom it was given to hurt the earth and the sea, Saying, Hurt not the earth, neither the sea nor the trees, till we have sealed the servants of our God in their foreheads.* (Rev 7:2-3)

So again the person, seen here as an angel, is ascending from the east. He has the seal or in other words the keys of the kingdom as we read before. He has the authority to command the angels who are commissioned to wreak natural havoc on the earth. In other words, he has the power of Elijah. Joseph Smith also received more information on this person:

> Q. *What are we to understand by the angel ascending from the east, Revelation 7th chapter and 2nd verse?*
>
> A. *We are to understand that the angel ascending from the east is he to whom is given the seal of the living God over the twelve tribes of Israel; wherefore, he crieth unto the four angels...And if you will receive it, this is Elias which was to come to gather the tribes of Israel and restore all things.* (D&C 77:9)

In this verse we have confirmed much of what we already know. He is Elias, or the precursor of the Savior; the harbinger or herald in Isaiah 41:27 above. And again we see his mission is to gather Israel pegging him as the same person in all these scriptures.

He holds the seal over the Tribes of Israel, or in other words he is the king and head of the priesthood, since he presides for the Lord, as we just read. So we have latter-day revelation confirming that these revelations in Isaiah and Revelation pertain to the last days and to the Davidic king who is to come. The Lord continues talking about his chosen servant:

> *My servant whom I sustain, my chosen one in whom I delight, him I have endowed with my Spirit; he will dispense justice to the nations. He will not shout or raise his voice to make himself heard in public. Even a bruised reed he will not break; a dim wick he will not snuff out. He will perform the work of justice in the cause of truth. Neither shall he himself grow dim or be bruised until he has brought about justice in the earth. The isles await his law. Thus says the Lord God, who frames and suspends the heavens, who gives form to the earth and its creatures, the breath of life to the people upon it, spirit to those who walk on it: I the Lord have rightfully called you and will grasp you by the hand; I have created you and appointed you to be a covenant for the people, a light to the nations, to open eyes that are blind, to free captives from confinement and from prison those who sit in darkness.* (Isaiah 42:1-7)

This is one of the most beautiful scriptures referring to the Davidic prophet/king. The Lord delights in this person and he is endowed with the spirit of the Lord. Because of this he is much like the Savior and Isaiah lists his attributes. Bruised reeds and dim wicks are metaphors for people. These metaphors refer to enemies, however. He will not kill wounded or disadvantaged enemies. He will perform justice and justice is one of his names.

In verses 6 and 7, the Lord speaks to his servant. This should dispel the notion that the subject of this prophecy is the Lord. It is clearly another. The Lord would not be speaking to himself in this way. In verse 5 he gives an affirmation of his godhood as the creator of the earth. Then in verses 6 and 7 he states that he, Jehovah the creator, has called him, the servant.

Grasping by the hand is the endowment of power and this function is very familiar to most of us. He is to be the living Davidic covenant in the last days. The Davidic covenant will be in force during the tribulation and will operate the same as in ancient times. This will be discussed later but suffice it here to say that this is the escape the Lord has prepared for the people. The members of the church will be taken captive, but he will free them from prison both in the literal and metaphorical senses under the terms of the Davidic covenant.

In Isaiah Chapters 41-55, he speaks much about the Davidic prophet and from these and the previous related verses, we get a picture of this man. Since this is the most important last days event for us, and our lives will depend on him, it is important to look at these scriptures, something that none of the other writers about the last days have done or been able to do.

> *I summon a bird of prey from the east, from a distant land the man who performs my counsel. What I have spoken, I bring to pass; what I have planned, I do. Hear me, you stubborn-hearted, who are far from righteousness; it is not now far off—my salvation shall no longer be delayed. I will grant deliverance in Zion, and to Israel my glory.* (Isaiah 46:11-13)

We are starting to read the same things again and again as the Lord introduces the king. Here he calls him a bird of prey as he will be to the Lord's enemies, but he summons him from the east from a distant land. Remember that he is speaking to us, the church in the United States so the land from where he comes, Palestine or Israel, is a distant land.

He then addresses us as stubborn-hearted who are far from righteousness. Righteousness is a name for the Davidic king, so he is talking about us who are far from him geographically at the moment, but we are also spiritually far from righteousness as we read in the first three chapters of Isaiah. We are in a state of apostasy today. But he says that righteousness is now, the time we are in, not far off and salvation will no longer be delayed. In other words we are there. This is the twelfth hour. The deliverance from captivity and the establishment of Zion in glory is at the door, therefore, the threatened captivity is even closer.

In another exciting passage, the Davidic prophet speaks in his own right:

> *Hear me, O isles; listen, you distant peoples: The Lord called me before I was in the belly; before I was in my mother's womb, he mentioned me by name. He has made*

my mouth like a sharp sword—in the shadow of his hand he hid me. He has made me into a polished arrow—in his quiver he kept me secret. He said to me, You are my servant, Israel, in whom I will be glorified. I had thought, I have labored in vain, I have spent my strength for nothing and to no purpose! Yet my cause rested with the Lord, my recompense with my God. For now the Lord has said—he who formed me from the womb to be his servant, to restore Jacob to him, Israel having been gathered to him; for I won honor in the eyes of the Lord when my god became my strength—he said: It is too small a thing for you to be my servant to raise up the tribes of Jacob and to restore those preserved of Israel. I will also appoint you to be a light to the nations, that my salvation may be to the end of the earth. Thus says the Lord, the Redeemer and Holy One of Israel, to him who is despised as a person, who is abhorred by his nation, a servant to those in authority: Rulers shall rise up when they see you, heads of state shall prostrate themselves, because the Lord keeps faith with you, because the Holy One of Israel has chosen you. Thus says the Lord: At a favorable time I have answered you; in the day of salvation I have come to your aid: I have created you and appointed you to be a covenant of the people, to restore the Land and reapportion the desolate estates, to say to the captives, Come forth! and to those in darkness, Show yourselves!... (Isaiah 49:1-9)

The Davidic prophet now speaks to us. Most have considered this to be another prophecy of the Christ but it clearly cannot be him. Nor is it Isaiah because this certainly does not apply to Isaiah's life and mission. In these verses we see his mission is the same as has been defined for the Davidic prophet in scriptures quoted earlier.

He says that before he was born, he was mentioned by name. Mother has two meanings. In addition to the literal, mother is also Zion or the church which is a central metaphor the Lord uses. We have always believed that all prophets received their calls before mortality but few are known before their birth.

Joseph Smith was mentioned in the Book of Mormon but this prophecy was unknown to anyone except the Nephites. It only came to light as far as we are concerned after Joseph was born and brought forth the record containing the prophecy. But because he was mentioned by name, many believed and some still do, that Joseph is the one who will return and do these things.

It cannot be Joseph for the simple reason that he is dead. There were witnesses to his death and burial. A few years ago the presidency of the RLDS church, to support their false claim to being prophets, supposedly revealed where Joseph and Hyrum were buried. They made a media show of the whole affair and there were many witnesses as they desecrated and dug up the resting place of the martyrs. They were both in the grave meaning that Joseph and Hyrum are not, or were not at that time, resurrected and were in fact dead. The only way Joseph could return and minister on earth would be as a resurrected celestial being and that is impossible. Celestial beings cannot or do not return to minister in the telestial world and do the things that the Davidic prophet is tasked to do. This pertains to those who are in mortality here.

There is only one other person who has been named specifically and this gives us the identity of the man. He is mentioned by Joseph Smith in DHC 6:253 quoted above, he is called by name in the Book of Mormon, he is referred to in Revelation which is explained in D&C 77:9, 14 where he is named, and Isaiah names him in 55:3. This same person is called by three different names indicative of his mission along with his given name, or the common name by which we know him. The Lord refers to him in Isaiah by one of his mission names:

> *Give ear and come unto me; pay heed, that your souls may live! And I will make with you an everlasting covenant: my loving fidelity toward David.* (Isaiah 55:3)

The covenant is the Davidic covenant which will be in effect and David here is not the ancient king but the modern Davidic prophet/king. As in 49:8 above, the Lord says "I have created you and appointed you to be a covenant of the people,..." This covenant is discussed in some detail in Isaiah 54 and elsewhere. (This entire book must be searched diligently as the Savior commanded in 3 Nephi 23:1-3.)

He is also mentioned in 1 Nephi 14:18-27 and called by his other given name which we will cover below. David is a title and all who occupy the seat of David are Davids. The Lord calls him Israel in this passage, although that is not his name. Israel means soldier of God and this is precisely what he is. He will battle the beast and his forces. He says his mouth is like a sharp sword and he is a polished arrow.

Another identifier is the fact that he has been hidden. The idea of a Davidic prophet has been unknown until the translation of Isaiah and the teaching of the manner of prophesying of the Jews. The book of Isaiah now makes clear that this great personage will in fact come. He was hidden in the shadow of his hand. This is again metaphorical and literal. This great man has been here for a long time but he has been hidden from our eyes. In addition, the knowledge of him has been hidden in the metaphorical language of this book. Hand is a metaphor for the Davidic prophet, hence, he has been hidden in the metaphor of hand and this was a secret until now. We can decipher the code in Isaiah and both identify him and see precisely what his mission is by reading what the "Hand" does. Had this been a prophecy of the Savior, it would not have been couched in secret, metaphorical terms so that no one could understand it until today.

There are other metaphorical names for the Davidic prophet: arm, sword, mouth, righteousness and justice. These also explain who he is and his mission. The Lord tells him that through his great last days mission, the Lord will be glorified in his servant.

Verses 4 and 5 give us a look at the thinking of the prophet before he embarks on his last-days mission. He says that he felt as though he had labored in vain spending his strength to no purpose. This is a very human reaction to the apparent desire to serve and work but without a specific mission. He has labored hard, apparently, but he trusted in the Lord to give him what he deserved. After these words, the Lord speaks to him and empowers him. His task is to restore Jacob to him. In Isaiah, Jacob is the name the Lord uses to refer to the Jews. At times he calls them Judah when he does not want to hide the meaning. But Jacob means the Ten Tribes as well. In this case, his mission is to restore the Ten Tribes. At the time he receives this duty or calling, Israel is already gathered to him. This is strange unless we understand that Israel is the name the Lord uses in Isaiah to refer to Ephraim or the church. Ephraim has been gathered through our missionary efforts and exists as the church today. This gives us a rough time check. The Davidic prophet will come after the church is organized and Ephraim is gathered and before the Ten Tribes are restored . That window is now. Since he has not come as of this writing, the time of his coming must be between today and the time when the Ten Tribes return which is immediately following the tribulation (the center of the last days chart).

The Lord empowers him in verse 5 and in verse 6 the Lord defines additional duties. He says it is not enough just to raise up the tribes of Jacob and restore the preserved of Israel (those who survive the tribulation). The Lord appoints him to be a light to the nations. This means he will yet preach to many nations and offer the Lord's salvation to all the world one last time.

We get another insight into his life in the last three verses. First, he is despised as a person and by his own nation. We know that he will be a Jew of the royal Davidic line, but he is abhorred by his people. This probably also refers to his coming to the church where he will be rejected by most of the members of the church because they know nothing of him since he was hidden in the shadow of the Lord's hand and because there was no teaching in the church about this great prophet. People in the church cannot understand Isaiah and therefore they cannot find out for themselves. In addition, as pointed out above, the official church position today is that stated by McConkie and adhered to by most CES scholars in the church, that there will be no Davidic prophet. When he comes then, people will say that he cannot be legitimate since he did not come through the traditional channels, i.e., be called as an apostle then outlive all of them. It is easy to see that only by either prior knowledge of him, as revealed in Isaiah and covered in this work, or by personal revelation will he be known. Since most people will reject him out of hand without seeking revelation, he will generally be rejected. This official but false doctrine, or rather, those who promote it, are the stumbling blocks spoken of above.

When he is empowered and assumes his rightful position, however, heads of state will bow down to him since all kingdoms will become subject to the Kingdom of Israel and to the king, David. He will be in difficult straits as is indicated here, but the Lord comes to his aid. In chapter 52, we will see some of the troubles he has to deal with.

One new task is mentioned in this reference. The Lord reiterates his calling to free the captives but says that he will restore the land and reapportion the desolate estates. This means that he will restore Israel to the lands of their inheritances and reapportion the lands to the tribes.

The Davidic prophet continues speaking:

My Lord the Lord has endowed me with a learned tongue, that I may know how to preach to those grown weary a word to wake them up. Morning by morning he wakens my ear to hear, as at study; my Lord the Lord has opened my ear, and I rebel not, nor back away: I offered my back to smiters, my cheeks to those who plucked out the beard; I hid not my face from insult and spitting. Because my Lord the Lord helps me, I shall not be disgraced; I have set my face like flint, knowing I shall not be confounded. He who vindicates me is near me. Who has a dispute with me? Let us face one another! Who will bring charges against me? Let him confront me with them! See my Lord the Lord sustains me. Who then will incriminate me? Surely all such shall wear out like a garment; the moth shall consume them. (Isaiah 50:4-9)

We learn some additional things about him. All the trials and tribulations, the acts and deeds of the prophet will serve as means to help identify him when he comes. First he has a learned tongue to arouse those (us) who have grown weary and fallen asleep. The dreary, repetitious preaching we are subjected to today in our meetings, will be replaced by the message of this great leader. He has plenty to say because the Lord wakes him every morning as though he were a student and speaks in his ear. We have had no such person since Joseph Smith. Imagine the flood of wonderful new knowledge that will be available from him.

But all will not be well with him. He will have to suffer some tough times. He is taken and whipped, tortured and suffers insult and spitting. But, like the Lord, he endures all because he knows his mission and he trusts in the Lord. He protests that he is guiltless and his torturers will turn to dust in the end.

When we examine his continued suffering in Isaiah 52, we will discuss the nature of the Davidic covenant and the need for such suffering. But before going to that chapter, there is one additional reference to examine. The Lord is speaking:

> *My righteousness shall be at hand and my salvation proceed; my arms shall judge the peoples—the isles anticipate me, awaiting my arm. Hear me, you who know righteousness, O people in whose heart is my law: Do not fear the reproach of men; be undaunted by their ridicule... But my righteousness shall endure forever,... Awake, arise; clothe yourself with power, O arm of the Lord! Bestir yourself, as in ancient times, as in generations of old. Was it not you who carved up Rahab, you who slew the dragon? Was it not you who dried up the Sea, the waters of the mighty deep, and made of ocean depths a way by which the redeemed might pass? Let the ransomed of the Lord return! Let them come singing to Zion, their heads crowned with everlasting joy; let them obtain joy and gladness, and sorrow and sighing flee away.* (Isaiah 5, 9-11)

Righteousness is a name for the Davidic prophet and salvation is the Savior. The two are at hand. The Lord also defines the metaphor "arm." He says that his two arms shall judge the people. These are the beast or antichrist, the king of Assyria and the Davidic prophet. His first (left) arm brings the people into captivity because of their idolatry and apostasy. The right arm is the one who frees the people and saves those who repent and are worthy. All people are in captivity along with Ephraim or the church. The isles, which are the people of the earth, are waiting for the Davidic king and to be saved from the archtyrant. He says my righteousness shall not fail and shall endure forever. He will not be defeated and will rule on the throne of Israel forever.

He also addresses the members of the church, the righteous remnant, who recognize and follow the Davidic king. He encourages them to be undaunted by the ridicule of men which will be renewed in these times. At the moment, there is little shame in being considered a faithful member of the church but that will change. The same forces that torture and abuse the Davidic king, will do so to his followers. Many of the abusers will be fellow members of the church. This sort of spiritual abuse is already beginning to be seen in the church.

The most revealing of these verses are 9-11 which give us a

picture of some premortal deeds performed by the Davidic king. The Lord addresses him, "O arm of the Lord!" He tells him to bestir himself as he did in ancient times. This would have to be in premortality. The Lord says that it was he who carved up Rehab. In Isaiah, this is ancient Egypt. The term Egypt in Isaiah always refers to the United States so when he wants to talk about ancient Egypt he uses another term, Rehab.

We know from other scriptures, which we will not cover in this work, that the Angel of His Presence, went with the people on the original exodus and was the power behind Moses. In Isaiah 63:9, he is also identified as that person: "with all their troubles he troubled himself, the angel of his presence delivering them." This is a very important revelation because it identifies the Davidic king, who is now mortal, is and was the famous Angel of His Presence or in other words, the angel who announces the presence of the Lord. This famous being has been active throughout the history of the world in his premortal state. This is not Gabriel, by the way. But this angel was the one who delivered the children of Israel from Egyptian captivity and he is now commissioned to free modern Israel from the captivity of the king of Assyria. He is also the last angel who appeared to Daniel. He had the power of Elijah over the elements during the original exodus too. This description is unmistakable and leaves no room for error or misinterpretation when all the parts of the prophecy are described.

The Lord will cause his ransomed people to be led to Zion and there they will be crowned with glory, be translated and have their call and election made sure.

In the next couple of chapters we get some additional detail although we pretty much know what his mission is from the several scriptures we have examined so far.

> *Then shall they say, How comely upon the mountains are the feet of the messenger announcing peace, who brings tidings of good, who heralds salvation, saying to Zion, Your God reigns! Hark! Your watchmen lift up their voice; as one they cry out for joy: before their very eyes they see the Lord's return to Zion. The Lord has bared his holy arm in the eyes of all nations, that all ends of the earth may see our God's salvation.* (Isaiah 52:7-8, 10)

This has been a traditional missionary encomium and was

made famous in a beautiful hymn sung by Jesse Evans Smith, the wife of President Joseph Fielding Smith. The picture conjured by the song are of missionaries scaling the mountains of the world but as usual, we fail to read and understand the entire message. Of course we can apply the scriptures to any meaning we wish, and people do it. But most scriptures, and certainly apocalyptic or prophetic scriptures have particular meanings.

Among literary scholars and critics there is a term called the intentional fallacy which states that any attempt to try to interpret a literary work in terms of what the author intended is a fallacy. A work of literary art should be enjoyed for what it is and not for what someone intended it to be. There is no intentional fallacy with the Lord's prophetic statements. We must understand what he meant specifically, since they are not works of art but works which are designed to convey the mysteries of God in metaphorical as well as literal expression.

In this prophecy the Lord is announcing his great last days prophet. We have to remember that mountains are nations, hence the messenger (singular) is going among the nations announcing peace and salvation. In other words, he is calling people to come to see the literal coming of the Lord. He announces the presence of the Lord. Peace and salvation are two names of the Savior.

After leading the captives to freedom, righteous Zion cries out for joy and the Savior returns to Zion. This is not his second coming which is a few years off. This takes place after the tribulation at the midpoint of the last days chart and in the land of Zion, Jackson County.

We know this is the Davidic prophet because the Lord says "he has bared his holy arm in the eyes of all nations." He is also the herald of salvation or of the Lord. He is both the Angel of His Presence and Elias who announces the Lord. Joseph identifies him as Elias in D&C 77. The Lord announces or introduces his prophet/king who then announces the presence of the Lord. The description continues:

> *My servant, being astute, shall be highly exalted; he shall become exceedingly eminent: just as he appalled many—his appearance was marred beyond human likeness, his semblance unlike that of men—So shall he yet astound many nations, rulers shutting their mouths at him—what*

was not told them, they shall see; what they had not heard, they shall consider. (Isaiah 52:13-15)

The Lord promises to make the Davidic prophet/king eminent and exalted. This is speaking in the literal sense of this world as well as eternal, but first he has to suffer because he is a righteous Davidic king. This citation gives us an idea of how he suffers. His suffering is almost equal to that of the Savior. We are told that he is tortured so badly that his appearance is no longer human. This is so bizarre and frightening that it is hard to read, much less imagine. More about this later.

After his suffering, he is healed and astounds many nations, and rulers will give him awed silence. There is no person since the Savior himself who has commanded such respect and recognition by the great of the world. In fact, the Savior did not receive much acclaim because he died. His mission was to give his life. The Davidic prophet has a mission that requires that he remain alive. In the days of ancient Israel, the people were put under covenant, which we call the Sinai covenant. This covenant required all men of Israel, without exception, to be righteous. This ideal is hardly achievable. An example is today in the church where only about 15 percent have temple recommends, which means only that number are complying with the most basic requirements, the same requirements as for baptism.

Israel was not able to comply with this covenant either and protection under the terms of the covenant was no longer given. The Lord then made another covenant with the people. This was the Davidic covenant, named after David, the first righteous king under this covenant.

The terms of the Davidic covenant are that Israel would be accepted by the Lord and he would shelter and protect them. He would give them power over their enemies and cause them to prosper in the land. What was required of the people was that the King be righteous and that the people obey him. There were few righteous Davidic kings in the history of ancient Israel. In fact most were very wicked causing the covenant to be out of force throughout most of the history of Israel. Josiah and Hezekiah were righteous kings. For this reason, the history of Hezekiah is found in the Book of Isaiah in Chapters 36-39. One prominent church writer called these chapters "useless historical detail."

Isaiah 36-39 show the comportment of a righteous Davidic king and how he must suffer to provide temporal salvation for his people. Hezekiah's suffering is detailed and although brief, the description gives us an idea of his physical and emotional agony. Each Davidic king must suffer as an offering or sacrifice to merit the covenant blessing. He suffers so that his people need not if they honor and obey him.

The Savior was a Davidic king although he was not allowed to occupy the throne he deserved. His atonement, however, was greater than that of an ordinary Davidic king because his sacrifice was to pay for the sin of Adam and for all sins under any covenant as the price for salvation. For this reason he had to die. But the suffering is the same. A condition of the suffering, however, is that it must be voluntary and unmerited.

The modern Davidic prophet must pay the price of releasing Israel from captivity and of providing temporal salvation during the tribulation and judgment periods. This suffering is so severe that he will not be recognizable as a human and people will be appalled at the sight, but he will not die and will be healed. Indeed, when we discover who he is, we will see he cannot die.

A very revealing description of this type of life is given by Isaiah to compare the lives and sacrifices of the Savior and of the modern Davidic prophet:

> *Who has believed our revelation? On whose account has the arm of the Lord been revealed? Like a sapling he grew up in his presence, a stalk out of arid ground. He had no distinguished appearance, that we should notice him; he had no pleasing aspect, that we should find him attractive. He was despised and disdained by men, a man of grief, accustomed to suffering. As one from whom men hide their faces he was shunned, deemed by us of no merit. Yet he bore our sufferings, endured our griefs, though we thought him stricken, smitten of God, and humbled. But he was pierced for our transgressions, crushed because of our iniquities; the price of our peace he incurred, and with his wounds we are healed. We all like sheep had gone astray, each of us headed his own way; the Lord brought together upon him the iniquity of us all. He was harassed, yet submissive, and opened not his mouth—like a lamb led to*

slaughter, like a sheep, dumb before its shearers, he opened not his mouth. By arrest and trial he was taken away. Who can apprise his generation that he was cut off from the land of the living for the crime of my people, to whom the blow was due? He was appointed among the wicked in death, among the rich was his burial; yet he had done no violence, and deceit was not in his mouth. But the Lord willed to crush him, causing him suffering, that, if he made his life an offering for guilt, he might see his offspring and prolong his days, and that the purposes of the Lord might prosper in his hand. He shall see the toil of his soul and be satisfied; because of his knowledge, and by bearing their iniquities, shall my servant, the righteous one, vindicate many. I will assign him an inheritance among the great, and he shall divide the spoil with the mighty, because he poured out his soul unto death, and was numbered with criminals—he bore the sins of many, and made intercession for the transgressors. (Isaiah 53:1-12)

I hate to be a complete iconoclast but again we have a well-known scripture which has been quoted many times from the KJV as a prophecy of the Savior describing his life. But as the Lord says in the first verse, he is talking about the arm who is the Davidic prophet. The same things apply generally to the Savior, however, but its purpose is to show that the Davidic king is a legitimate one and undergoes such severe suffering that he is like the Savior. He is a messiah who will save many people in the last days.

He grew up and was not distinguished in any respect. As a man, he is despised and disdained by men. But because of the sufferings he endured, he paid for transgressions of the people and they are saved as a result of his wounds. Isaiah is using the editorial "we" referring to Israel and especially Ephraim or the church. We are in apostasy and like sheep have wandered afield.

We have to remember that this book is talking about our time and is not a prophecy of the Savior who has already come. But Isaiah uses what are called types from the past to show the future: "Who predicts what happens as do I, and is the equal of me in appointing a people from of old as types, foretelling things to come?" (Isaiah 44:7). So the descriptions, though they may be of another person or people in past times, are used to show what is going to be repeated or done in our time. So this description of the Savior shows the same suffering and persecution that the Davidic prophet will undergo, except that he will not die.

In the last two verses of this passage, the Lord tells us that he is speaking of the Davidic prophet. Earlier, we read of the anguish the Davidic prophet felt because he thought he had wasted his strength, that is moral and spiritual strength, without any purpose. This is the toil of the soul and here the Lord says he will be satisfied and receive his recompense, part of which is to vindicate many. The Lord calls him "my servant, the righteous one." The Lord recognizes and accepts his sacrifice on behalf of many, not all as did the Savior, but he made intercession in the Davidic covenantal sense. Who can fail to appreciate this great leader the Lord has prepared for our last-days survival?

One final look at the prophecies about the Davidic prophet in Isaiah should suffice to convince even the most skeptical of the reality of this great personage:

> *Hark, a tumult from the city, a noise from the temple! It is the voice of the Lord paying his enemies what is due them. Before she is in labor, she gives birth; before her ordeal overtakes her, she delivers a son! Who has heard the like, or who has seen such things? Can the earth labor but a day and a nation be born at once? For as soon as she was in labor, Zion gave birth to her children. Shall I bring to a crisis and not bring on birth? says the Lord. When it is I who cause the birth, shall I hinder it? says your God.* (Isaiah 66:6-9)

Here is a riddle the Lord gives us and it is only by much study and a thorough knowledge of the scriptures of the last days that we are able to understand it. For many years we have misinterpreted these marvelous revelations, sometimes making them more complicated, but usually oversimplifying them and not caring whether all parts of the metaphor fit together and make sense.

The only part of this scripture that pertains to the Davidic prophet is verse 7. This tells us that she gives birth before she is in labor and the second line is a parallel saying the same thing, that she delivers a son before her ordeal overtakes her.

The question is, who is "she?" The son is the Davidic prophet and he is delivered before the woman is in labor. Although this cannot be done in real life, it is possible in metaphor. The woman is the common metaphor for the church and the son is one of the offspring we discussed earlier, albeit a most important one, if not the most important ever.

The labor is the tribulation which comes upon the church in our time. This gives us an important time check too. The son or Davidic prophet comes along before the tribulation (labor) or invasion by the beast, the king of Assyria. On the last days chart, I have shown the rise of the beast and of the Davidic prophet both occurring at the beginning of the tribulation period. They occur at about the same time and we will look at this further.

The riddle continues by saying that when the woman goes into labor, she labors only a day and a nation is born at once. She gives birth to her children in one day. The prophet asks the question if the earth is able to labor only one day and bring forth a nation. The answer, of course, is no! But the woman does it.

The Lord then asks if it is logical that he bring on the labor, or crisis which is the tribulation, and not give birth. Since he is the one causing the birth, he will not hinder it. We will come back to this riddle because it is the third major event of the last days and will be covered fully in the next chapter. For now, let us finish our search for the Davidic prophet and discover who he is.

There is also a verse in Revelation which pictures the same riddle and speaks of the manchild being born to the woman:

> *And there appeared a great wonder in heaven, a woman clothed with the sun, and the moon under her feet, and upon her head a crown of twelve stars. And she being with child cried, travailing in birth, and pained to be delivered. And she brought forth a man child, who was to rule all nations with a rod of iron: and her child was caught up unto God and his throne.* (Rev 12:1-2, 5)

(The number and order of the verses follow Joseph Smith's order because the verse order in the KJV is incorrect.) The same thing is seen in this vision. The woman gives birth to a man child who is to rule all nations with a rod of iron. The woman has been identified, by the easily recognizable symbols given her, as the church. There is no argument on this and it is obvious and correct. But who is the man child?

In the days when I was a missionary, we used this scripture to show that there had been an apostasy of the original church of Jesus Christ. The man child was thought to be the priesthood which was taken to heaven and the woman fled into the wilderness representing the going into apostasy. But I now know from Isaiah that this vision pertains to the last days. We will discuss it in the next chapter, but the man child is the same as the son in Isaiah 66 who is the Davidic prophet. Joseph Smith defined the child as the "kingdom." Joseph received the revelation in D&C 113 wherein the Lord says he, the Davidic prophet, will hold the keys of the kingdom. So they are one and the same and Joseph used "kingdom" since he was hidden and the Davidic prophet is the kingdom. Joseph probably knew that as well as the fact that he was to remain hidden until just before his appearance.

To summarize a little, we know several things about the mission of the Davidic prophet from Isaiah and the other scriptures cited in this section:

1. His primary mission is to gather the scattered of Israel; the Ten Tribes. (Isaiah 49:5-7
2. He will be the living covenant, which is the Davidic royal calling. (Isaiah 42:6, 49:6)
3. He will sit on the throne of David and rule his kingdom, Israel, forever. (Isaiah 9:7)
4. He will free the captives of Israel. (Isaiah 49:9-10)
5. He will lead the people of Israel to Zion and will apportion the lands of their inheritance. (Isaiah 49:8)
6. He will be a light to the nations. (Isaiah 42:6)
7. He is the Lord's herald or harbinger. (Isaiah 40:3, 41:27)
8 He will preside over the church/kingdom. (Isaiah 40:10)
9. He is the one the Lord loves. (Isaiah 48:14-15)
10. He was named before he was born. (Isaiah 49:1-2)
11. He rightly holds the keys of the priesthood and kingdom. (D&C 113:4-6)
12. He was with Moses on the original exodus as the Angel of his Presence and afterward. (Isaiah 51:9-11; 37:36; 48:13-16; 63:9; D&C 133:53)
13. He is a descendant of Jesse and also partly of Ephraim. (Isaiah 11:1; D&C 113:3-6)

14. He comes from the east, meaning the Middle East, or from the land today called Israel but which is really Judah. (Isaiah 41:2; 46:11; Rev 7:2)
15. He is the king of Israel. (Isaiah 9:7; D&C 77:9)
16. He will restore all things. (D&C 77:9)

This is a very big order and looking at the list (and there is more) to call him the one mighty and strong is an understatement. There is much more to his mission, at least as far as details of his actions go. And he has one very important function which will be covered in the next chapter. At this time we need to identify him.

> Q. *What are we to understand by the angel ascending from the east...*
>
> A. *We are to understand that the angel ascending from the east is he to whom is given the seal of the living God over the twelve tribes of Israel;... And if you will receive it, this is Elias which was to come to gather together the tribes of Israel and restore all things.* (D&C 77:9)

This verse was quoted and discussed above. The important item herein as far as identification, is that the Lord, through Joseph Smith, identifies this person as Elias. This is a title, however, and not a name. Later John sees more:

> *And I took the little book out of the angel's hand, and ate it up; and it was in my mouth sweet as honey: and as soon as I had eaten it, my belly was bitter. And he said unto me, Thou must prophesy again before many peoples, and nations, and tongues, and kings.* (Rev 10:10)
>
> Q. *What are we to understand by the little book which was eaten by John, as mentioned in the 10th chapter of Revelation?*
>
> A. *We are to understand that it was a mission, and an ordinance, for him to gather the tribes of Israel; behold this is Elias, who, as it is written, must come and restore all things.* (D&C 77:14)

The identification is now complete. John's mission in the last days is to gather the tribes of Israel and be the forerunner of the Savior. He is to preach before many nations and kings. This is the calling of the Davidic prophet and so we have identified this great being. For this important mission John has tarried in the flesh preparing himself for 19 centuries. Who else is more worthy? Who else has the right to the keys of the priesthood and of the kingdom? He already holds them. He was ordained by the Savior himself and is senior to all living apostles. All that is required of him to legitimately preside, is to appear. He need not be appointed or called by the then presiding officers of the church because he is already appointed.

This is a marvelous revelation. People have had no idea what John's work would be in the last days. Even though the answer has been here all the time, we have not been able to understand the Book of Isaiah until it was correctly translated and we learned something about the manner of prophesying of the Jews. Now we know for whom to look. In Revelation, John is seeing his own mission and the things that will take place during this period.

> *And there was given me a reed like unto a rod: and the angel stood, saying, Rise, and measure the temple of God, and the altar, and them that worship therein. But the court which is without the temple leave out, and measure it not; for it is given unto the Gentiles: and the holy city shall they tread under foot forty and two months.* (Rev 11:1-2)

Another prophecy the members are familiar with is that the temple will be rebuilt in Old Jerusalem. It is well known that the Jews have already started accumulating the materials and have prepared the temple vessels and instruments to once again begin the temple sacrifices and ordinances. Some wonder why the temple has not been started since they are quite prosperous. Part of the problem is that they do not know exactly how it should be done. Of course the major problem is that the Palestinians control the temple mount. They have their Dome of the Rock and the El Aqsa Mosque there. The Jews not only need guidance but need that holy site returned to their control.

In these verses, the angel gives John a measuring rod and tells him to measure the temple, etc. In other words, John is being commissioned to direct the building of the temple in the last days. This is another important and vital calling we did not know about before. We get some additional detail from another obscure reference, which no one has previously been able to decipher correctly, found in Daniel:

> *Seventy weeks are determined upon thy people and upon*

> *the holy city, to finish the transgression, and to make an end of sins, and to make reconciliation for iniquity, and to bring in everlasting righteousness, and to seal up the vision and prophecy, and to anoint the most Holy. Know therefore and understand, that from the going forth of the commandment to restore and to build Jerusalem unto the Messiah the Prince shall be seven weeks, and threescore and two weeks: the street shall be built again, and the wall, even in troublous times. And after threescore and two weeks shall Messiah be cut off, but not for himself: and the people of the prince that shall come shall destroy the city and the sanctuary; and the end thereof shall be with a flood, and unto the end of the war desolations are determined. And he shall confirm the covenant with many for one week: and in the midst of the week he shall cause the sacrifice and the oblation to cease, and for the overspreading of abominations he shall make it desolate, even until the consummation, and that determined shall be poured upon the desolate.* (Dan 9:24-27)

The ninth chapter of Daniel is mostly a prayer of confession and begging forgiveness for the sins of his people. At the outset he says that he read in Jeremiah that Jerusalem would be desolate for 70 years (Jeremiah 25:12). He had previously asked, and will do so again, how long the Jews are going to have to suffer captivity. Apparently he received the answer from Jeremiah's writings and by some inspiration because Jeremiah did not exactly say this.

Gabriel, however, appears to him again and says that he is going to explain some things to him and give him understanding. What he does is give another riddle. Daniel protests up to the end that he still does not understand. This is because the revelations are being given for us in the last days, as the angel explains to Daniel at the end of his record. "Go thy way, Daniel: for the words are closed up and sealed till the time of the end." (Dan 12:9). This tells us that these prophecies were not for Daniel and the Jews at that time, but rather, for us today. One of these is the quote from Daniel 9 above.

The seventy weeks have been explained in different ways by the few who have attempted to explain them. Some have tried to affix some mystical time to the 70 weeks, or to equate it with

Jeremiah's 70 years. The amazing thing we have discovered is that all definite times the Lord gives are literal times. The 1260, 1335, and 1290 days in Daniel are literal and so are the 70 weeks.

This prophecy takes place at the end of the tribulation period, or the first three-and-a-half years on the last days chart. It is the last 70 weeks of this period.

During the tribulation, the entire world is conquered by the beast, the king of Assyria including the land of the Jews which they call Israel. The Lord provides a period of respite of 70 weeks beginning a little over two years into the tribulation. The respite, according to Gabriel, is to allow the Jews to end their transgression, repent and accept the Savior, Jesus the Christ. There is a nice little metaphor here which you should by now pick up on. The Jews are to bring in everlasting righteousness, which we know to be the Davidic prophet, since righteousness is his name, and they do bring him in initially.

In verse 25, Gabriel goes on to say that from the time the Davidic prophet, who we know to be John, receives the command to rebuild Jerusalem, which is largely destroyed after two years of war, it is 69 weeks until the streets and wall are rebuilt in troublous times. We know from Revelation 7:2 that John is also commanded to rebuild the temple, although Gabriel does not mention it. This commandment is given to "Messiah the Prince." This is not the Savior because no one is giving him commandments so Messiah the Prince must be someone else which we know him to be. He is the prince or king of Israel. He is called messiah because he is Israel's temporal savior and they see him as such. He is fully empowered at this time and has control over the elements and over the invaders as well.

The people gladly accept him as the Messiah because he precisely fits their picture of the Jewish Messiah. He is a legitimate Davidic king and powerful being, translated, with full power and he protects them from their enemies. They rejoice at his presence and joyfully accept him as their king. After 62 weeks, however, the Jews do the unthinkable; they reject Messiah the Prince, or as it says here, they cut him off.

There is a note at the end that says, "...but not for himself:" In other words, they do not reject him for who he is but for some other reason. This reason, as you may well imagine, is because he is preaching another messiah, Jesus the Christ whom the Jews will not accept. In spite of the great wonders he performs, rebuilding the city, the streets and even the temple and holding the beast at bay, they will not accept the one who empowers him. Such stubbornness is incomprehensible.

There are many, however, who do repent and accept the Savior and enter into the Davidic covenant. He confirms the covenant, that is, he seals them in the covenant during a week-long effort. These converts are then taken to join the saints in the US on the exodus, which we will discuss in the next chapter, so they are able to escape the results of their folly.

What follows is not pretty. The "people of the prince" are the soldiers of the king of Assyria who enter the city and destroy both the city and the sanctuary or temple. The people come as a flood. This is a metaphor for moving people as explained above, and moving people are an army. So an army enters Jerusalem and makes it desolate until the end of the war, which, luckily is only a few weeks away.

In the last verse of this citation it says "...he shall cause the sacrifice and the oblation to cease." It sounds as though the Davidic prophet is causing it to cease but this is the king of Assyria. The language is a little confusing here with too many "hes" in the same phrase. When the king of Assyria invades, he puts an end to the sacrifice, naturally, because he desecrates and overruns the temple and the city. Since he makes all people worship him through the false religion set up by the second beast, or false prophet, he will tolerate no other worship, especially any devotions which pertain to the true God. The city and temple will remain in this state until the consummation of the abomination of desolation is poured out.

With the end of the 70 weeks, the tribulation period ends because the king of Assyria is destroyed in the US where other events take place at the beginning of the seventh seal. There is likely a short period of quiet after the tyrant is destroyed and people throughout the world will try to get their lives in order again. During the reign of the antichrist, millions of people were annihilated. As happens in war, families are separated, some are killed and never heard of again. During this period, people will return to their own countries. In the tribulation and conquest of the world the king of Assyria abolished borders:

But when my Lord has fully accomplished his work in Mount Zion and in Jerusalem, he will punish the king of Assyria for his notorious boasting and infamous conceit, because he has said, I have done it by my own ability and shrewdness, for I am ingenious. I have done away with the borders of nations, I have ravaged their reserves, I have vastly reduced the inhabitants. I have impounded the wealth of peoples like a nest, and I have gathered up the whole world as one gathers abandoned eggs; not one flapped its wings, or opened its mouth to utter a peep.(Isaiah 10:12-14)

Then, like a deer that is chased, or a flock of sheep that no one rounds up, each will return to his own people and everyone flee to his homeland. (Isaiah 13:14)

The mission of the Davidic prophet is ended among the Jews and he returns to the land of Zion for the midterm events and to continue his mission which is entering its second phase.

In this section we have looked at the prophecies foretelling the coming of the Davidic prophet/king in the last days. In these prophecies, we also learned of the many duties of his majestic calling. But we did not examine all the events in which he will participate. This book is divided into the five major events of the last days and as we look at the major events, we will see the Davidic prophet participating and directing them.

The Exodus And The Birth Of Zion

By far the most important, exciting and miraculous event of the last days is something that few members of the church even know about and it is certainly not discussed in any of the current crop of last-days commentaries. Yet this is the central event pertaining to the righteous members of the church and it will only affect members of the church. This event is the last-days exodus.

The reason it is not understood or even known about is that the majority of scriptures having to do with the exodus are highly metaphorical. The metaphors trip most commentators up because they have not learned the method of interpreting them, so they wind up with erroneous interpretations, which, unfortunately hang around the church for decades. After many years, if no one of authority has made better or later interpretations, the originals become canonized by default and then if one tries to reinterpret them, he is looked at as a heretic at best. But truth will out and we will look at the prophecies of the exodus in their true meanings, and perhaps this may ultimately save your life, which is really my goal. As before, we will begin this section by looking at what Isaiah has to say, then we will cover the other prophecies:

Come, O my people, enter your chambers and shut the doors behind you; hide yourselves a little while until the wrath is past. (Isaiah 26:20)

The things of the past are types of future events. Here we see the last days Passover. When the tribulation begins, the Lord counsels the righteous who are prepared, to enter their chambers, or homes, and shut the doors until the wrath passes over. This is the same commandment given to the Israelites as they prepared to leave ancient Egypt. It will be the same today. In order to enter into our chambers and shut the doors to wait out the initial tribulation, we will have to have enough food. Those who do not, will have to leave their homes and scavenge for food for their families. This will put them in mortal danger and they will be killed by the invading troops. There is more to say about this later, but the exodus is metaphorically revealed in Revelation which we looked at briefly:

And there appeared a great wonder in heaven; a woman clothed with the sun, and the moon under her feet, and upon her head a crown of twelve stars: And she being with child cried, travailing in birth, and pained to be delivered. And there appeared another wonder in heaven; and behold a great red dragon, having seven heads and ten horns, and seven crowns upon his heads. And his tail drew the third part of the stars of heaven, and did cast them to the earth: and the dragon stood before the woman which was ready to be delivered, for to devour her child as soon as it was born. And she brought forth a man child, who was to rule all nations with a rod of iron: and her child was caught up unto God, and to his throne. And the woman fled into the wilderness, where she hath a place prepared of God, that they should feed her there a thousand two hundred and threescore days. (Rev 12:1-6)

We discussed this vision in the last part of the previous section. This great vision is depicted on the cover. The woman is the church and the man child is the Davidic prophet whom the dragon wants to destroy as soon as he appears. The last verse says that the woman fled into the wilderness where God has prepared a place for her to be fed for 1260 days or three-and-a-half years, equal to the time the beast has power and the duration of the tribulation.

This wonderful metaphorical vision has not been interpreted correctly in this dispensation at least. For many years it was taught that the woman fleeing into the wilderness was a metaphor for the apostasy of the primitive church. The great apostasy did occur, but this vision has nothing to do with it. It is a last-days vision. Slightly before the tribulation begins, the Davidic prophet appears. The beast wants to destroy him, or rather, Satan does, and he gives power to the beast. The king of Assyria probably does not know anything about him at this stage in his life because the Lord takes him out of the way for a time.

This vision spans the time between the time of John, who is the Davidic prophet, and the time when he comes to the church again. When he was "born" or was part of the church, he was translated and taken out of the reach of the dragon, but, he will also appear in the church at the time the beast arises again.

When the tribulation begins at the invasion of the world by the king of Assyria, or the antichrist, or the beast, all of whom are the same, the woman flees into the wilderness where she will remain until the tribulation is ended.

There is the belief, not based on any scripture, that says there will be a group of people called to go to Jackson County to begin building the New Jerusalem and the temple. Many people have moved there and bought property so they will already in place when the time comes. This is like going on a mission so you will be already in the field when you receive your call. Some I have talked to feel strongly that the Lord has inspired them to make the move. One cannot argue with inspiration, but what the scriptures say is that the land will be cleansed by the king of Assyria when he comes. That land will have to be redeemed by the shedding of blood and the manifestation of great power:

For after much tribulation, as I have said unto you in a former commandment, cometh the blessing. Behold, this is the blessing which I have promised after your tribulations, and the tribulations of your brethren—your redemption, and the redemption of your brethren, even their restoration to the land of Zion, to be established, no more to be thrown down. Nevertheless, if they pollute their inheritances they shall be thrown down; for I will not spare them if they pollute their inheritances. Behold, I say unto you, the redemption of Zion must needs come by power; Therefore, I will raise up unto my people a man, who shall lead them like as Moses led the children of Israel. (D&C 103:11-16)

The saints will have to pass through tribulation before they can be restored to the land of Zion. This is not talking about the saints of the 1830s but to us. We are the ones who are going to suffer the period the Lord calls the tribulation or the captivity of the king of Assyria. Why would anyone want to go to the land of Zion today before it has been redeemed and swept clean?

The man who is like Moses is the Davidic prophet as we showed earlier. The Davidic prophet will lead the people on the exodus back to New Jerusalem. The only people who will be in the land of Jackson County will be the beast and his soldiers because he sets up his North American headquarters there and there is where he will be destroyed:

And he shall plant the tabernacles of his palace between the seas in the glorious holy mountain; yet he shall come to his end, and none shall help him. (Dan 11:45)

Back to the exodus. The church has been taken into the wilderness but there are more details:

And to the woman were given two wings of a great eagle, that she might fly into the wilderness, into her place, where she is nourished for a time, and times, and half a time, from the face of the serpent. And the serpent cast out of his mouth water as a flood after the woman, that he might cause her to be carried away of the flood. And the earth helped the woman, and the earth opened her mouth, and swallowed up the flood which the dragon cast out of his mouth. And the dragon was wroth with the woman, and went to make war with the remnant of her seed, which keep the commandments of God, and have the testimony of Jesus Christ. (Rev 12:14-17)

We know that moving water is an army and here the dragon acting through the beast, sends a "flood" which is a large force to overcome the members who have been taken into the wilderness. We are seeing the events of the first exodus reenacted. Pharaoh sent an army to bring back or destroy the Israelites and his army was destroyed by a natural catastrophe caused by Moses' control over the elements. The same thing will happen in this last days exodus as the troops pursue the remnant and they will neither return nor be heard of again.

When his troops do not return, the dragon, Satan, is angry and causes his beast, the king of Assyria, to make war with the remnant of her seed. Here is another puzzle. If the church has gone into the wilderness, how can the beast make war with the remnant of her seed? We would expect that those who are wicked, or who do not want to be active in the church would be left behind, but this last verse says that he goes to make war with those who have testimonies of the Savior and who keep his commandments. So these people are righteous, hence, not all the righteous go on the exodus. But I am getting ahead. We need to continue looking at the taking of the church into the wilderness first. In verse 14, it says that she was given the wings of a great eagle with which she flies into the wilderness.

When the Savior was speaking to his disciples they wanted to know the signs of his coming and of the end of the world. He told them many things: there would be false Christs, wars and rumors of wars, famines and earthquakes, and the gospel would be preached in all the world for the last time. (Matthew 24). The chronology is all jumbled and out of order.

Luke gives a similar account but it is better, especially because Joseph Smith translated and corrected some of the verses:

> *And as it was in the days of Noe, so shall it be also in the days of the Son of man. They did eat, they drank, they married wives, they were given in marriage, until the day that Noe entered the ark, and the flood came, and destroyed them all. Likewise also as it was in the days of Lot; they did eat, they drank, they bought, they sold, they planted, they builded; But the same day that Lot went out of Sodom it rained fire and brimstone from heaven, and destroyed them all. Even thus shall it be in the day when the Son of*

man is revealed. In that day, he which shall be upon the housetop, and his stuff in the house, let him not come down to take it away: and he that is in the field, let him likewise not return back. Remember Lot's wife. Whosoever shall seek to save his life shall lose it; and whosoever shall lose his life shall preserve it. I tell you, in that night there shall be two men in one bed; the one shall be taken, and the other shall be left. Two women shall be grinding together; the one shall be taken, and the other left. Two men shall be in the field; the one shall be taken, and the other left. And they answered and said unto him, Where, Lord? And he said unto them, Wheresoever the body is, thither will the eagles be gathered together. (Luke 17:26-37)

The Savior is talking about the time just before the tribulation begins. In fact, he is talking about the time just before the civil war and unrest begin in the United States. He refers to his coming as the beginning of the days of tribulation and judgment so before he begins either, people are living pretty much as normal. But in one night at the beginning of the tribulation, there is a massive leaving of people: one from bed, one from the field, and so on. The disciples ask the obvious question, "Where are they taken?" The Lord answers with another riddle. He tells them that where the body is, the eagles will be gathered together. The Joseph Smith translation gives the explanation:

And they answered and said unto him, Where, Lord, shall they be taken. And he said unto them, Wheresoever the body is gathered; or, in other words, withersoever the saints are gathered, thither will the eagles be gathered together; or thither will the remainder be gathered together. Thus he spake, signifying the gathering of his saints; and of angels descending and gathering the remainder unto them; the one from the bed, the other from the grinding, and the other from the field, whithersoever he listeth. (Luke 17:36-38 JST)

This is the manner in which the exodus will take place. The eagle wings given to the woman are the angels who gather the righteous remnant in one night and transport them to the wilderness where the saints are collected into one body. Eagles refer to angels or to translated beings in Hebrew metaphorical language.

The eagles are also the righteous ones who are gathered out in this miraculous manner and taken to the wilderness. Isaiah says:

> *But they who hope in the Lord shall be renewed in strength: they shall ascend as on eagles wings; they shall run without wearying, they shall walk and not faint.* (Isaiah 40:31)

And:

> *Who are these, aloft like clouds, flying as doves to their portals?* (Isaiah 60:8)

This is the fulfillment of the promise in the oath and covenant of the priesthood. It is realized by those who are taken on the exodus because there will be the elderly, the infirm and the very young. All will be renewed in their bodies and translated during the course of the exodus. The gathering of the eagles will occur in one night or day, depending on which hemisphere you are in, so some will be in the fields while others will be sleeping. The righteous remnant who are to go on the exodus will be taken from the worthy members wherever they are in the world.

Unlike the first exodus, however, the people will not take any possessions or supplies. They will go in the clothing they are wearing and will not be allowed to go back for their "stuff." The Lord will provide for the people. He will place a canopy over them to protect from the sun and the other elements:

> *Over the whole site of Mount Zion, and over its solemn assembly, the Lord will form a cloud by day and a mist glowing with fire by night: above all that is glorious shall be a canopy. It shall be a shelter and shade from the heat of the day, a secret refuge from the downpour and from the rain.* (Isaiah 4:5-6)

Mount Zion is the nation of Zion formed in the day the exodus takes place. This is the puzzle cited earlier:

> *Before she is in labor, she gives birth; before her ordeal overtakes her, she delivers a son! Who has heard the like, or who has seen such things? Can the earth labor but a day and a nation be born at once? For as soon as she was in labor, Zion gave birth to her children. Shall I bring to a crisis and not bring on birth? says the Lord.* (Isaiah 66:7-9)

So we now can solve the riddle. The Davidic prophet was born before she was in labor, or before the tribulation began. But then the tribulation begins which is the labor of the woman in bringing forth her children. The labor lasts only one day and the nation is born at once. The exodus happens in one day at the beginning of the tribulation and the nation of Zion is created.

It is not clear how long the righteous remnant will have to endure the tribulation when it begins, but it will not be long because the exodus happens "as soon as she was in labor." This is a great comfort to the truly righteous remnant in the church because they will escape the captivity, or most of it, and the cruel oppression which the rest of the church will suffer throughout the world, especially in this country.

> *The sinners in Zion are struck with fear; the godless are in the grip of trembling: Who among us can live through the devouring fire? Who among us can abide eternal burning? They who conduct themselves righteously and are honest in word, who disdain extortion and stay their hand from taking bribes, who stop their ears at the mention of murder, who shut their eyes at the sight of wickedness. They shall dwell on high; the impregnable cliffs are their fortress. Bread is provided them, their water is sure. Your eyes shall behold the King in his glory and view the expanse of the earth. You shall recount in your mind the terror: Where are those who conducted the census? Where are those who levied the tax? Where are the ones who appraised the towers? The insolent people are not to be seen, a nation of incomprehensible speech, whose babbling tongue was unintelligible.* (Isaiah 33:14-19)

Isaiah describes the condition among the church members when the tribulation arrives. They are struck with fear and trembling. There are two dangers: the devouring fire, which is the king of Assyria and the eternal burning which is the Lord. Either way there is death. But he gives some of the attributes of those who can escape.

Those who are righteous will escape, that is, those who are not idolaters (seeking bribes and filling their heads with TV violence, murder and other wickedness). They who have these attributes and one other that we will mention, will go on the exodus which is described here. They will be taken to the wilderness, which is mountain country around here, where those on the exodus will be. The cliffs are impregnable and will be their fortress.

Perhaps the greatest blessing on the exodus will be the privilege of seeing the glorified Lord along with the Davidic prophet/king. The king spoken of here is probably the Davidic king but elsewhere the Lord says he will be with the people and they will see him. During this trek, the people will be taught both by the Davidic prophet and by the Lord.

In order to be in the presence of the Lord, one has to be translated and indeed, those who go on the exodus will be translated and during the 42 months of the exodus, they will have their call and election made sure.

While looking out over the earth amid the peace that exists in this company, the people will recall the terror of the king of Assyria, albeit brief, and will wonder where are the tax collectors etc. The babbling tongues of the invaders who spoke Russian and Chinese which were unintelligible to us, are no longer heard and are a fading memory.

The Lord will provide food and water during the trek:

> *But to you this will be a sign: This year eat what grows wild, and the following year what springs up of itself. But in the third year sow and harvest, plant vineyards and eat their fruit:...For out of Jerusalem shall go a remnant, and from Mount Zion a band of survivors. The zeal of the Lord of Hosts will accomplish it.* (Isaiah 37:30, 32)

It is unlikely that the people will eat manna because Isaiah says they will eat what springs up or grows wild which is the same thing, apparently. So for two years the people on the exodus will eat along the road whatever the Lord provides but the third year they will have reached the promised land, or Jackson County where they begin to plant and harvest. The city of Enoch will not have descended yet and the area will be barren. The power of the Davidic king will keep the archtyrant at bay and eventually, he will be destroyed there.

The band of survivors is descriptive of the situation. Survivors generally suggests that some tragedy took place and those who made it through, are the survivors. In this case, the small band of survivors left first and the rest remained to suffer the captivity and tribulation.

Although the exodus is discussed in many other places in Isaiah, one additional scripture should be enough to get a good picture of this wondrous happening:

Wilderness and arid land shall be jubilant; the desert shall rejoice when it blossoms like the crocus. Joyously it shall break out in flower, singing with delight; it shall be endowed with the glory of Lebanon, the splendor of Carmel and Sharon. The glory of the Lord and the splendor of our God they shall see there. Strengthen the hands grown feeble, steady the failing knees. Say to those with fearful hearts, Take courage, be unafraid! See, your God is coming to avenge and to reward; God himself will come and deliver you. Then shall the eyes of the blind be opened and the ears of the deaf unstopped. Then shall the lame leap like deer, and the tongue of the dumb shout for joy. Water shall break forth in the wilderness and streams flow in the desert. the land of mirages shall become one of lakes, the thirsty place springs of water; in the haunt of howling creatures shall marshes break out, in the reserves shall come rushes and reeds. There shall be highways and roads which shall be called the Way of Holiness, for they shall be for such as are holy, the unclean shall not traverse them; on them shall no reprobates wander. No lions shall be encountered there, nor shall wild beasts intrude. But the redeemed shall walk them, the ransomed of the Lord shall return; they shall come singing to Zion, their heads crowned with everlasting joy. (Isaiah 35:1-10)

This is another of the passages in Isaiah that commentators and teachers have mistakenly assumed to be a messianic prophecy. In fact this is a metaphorical picture of the exodus. The wilderness will blossom and break out in flower. This does not mean that vegetation will begin to grow. Flowers are people and blossoms are usually children. The glory of Lebanon is elite or redeemed Israel and Carmel and Sharon are parallel terms. In addition the glory and splendor of the Lord will be there. This is a marvelous epiphany.

The three verses talking about the hands being strengthened and the failing knees, the blind and deaf being healed, are miracles that will occur on the journey. Since the exodus will include elderly and handicapped people, they will have to be strengthened in order to participate in the trek, which will be on foot. The fact is that all will be healed of any infirmities they have. Their bodies will be renewed as we learned above. This is the fulfillment of the promise made in the oath and covenant of the priesthood.

Another blessing that will be realized is the healing of barren women. There has been a myth around the church for decades that says that those who have little children who die, will be able to raise them in the Millennium. This would amount to reincarnation which is a Hindu doctrine and is false.

Barren women who go on the exodus and others who come to Zion later, will be healed and have children in large numbers. There are women who have received blessings telling them they would have and raise children when these women are barren and some are now beyond their child-bearing age. The blessings, if they were inspired, will come true at this time. Children who died before accountability, however, are in the celestial worlds and during the Millennium, their mothers may have contact with them but they will be adult, resurrected beings.

The water, described as lakes and streams, is people as we have said. They are in the wilderness and the blossoming and greening of the desert is because the translated celestial people of Zion are there.

The roads will be called holy because the holy people, the redeemed, are on them. These roads will also later be used for the final gathering of the righteous. The Lord also says there will be no lions there or other wild beasts. These are metaphors for men also. They are soldiers or mobs, but none will be seen here.

The final verse is glorious in its message. The ransomed will return to the place called Zion, in Jackson County where they are crowned with everlasting joy. Singing is a metaphor for worship and there will be a new kind of worship at this time. The crowning with everlasting joy means that they are sealed up to exaltation by the Holy Spirit of Promise, who is the Savior.

There are many other scriptures in Isaiah which describe the exodus and give more details about it and the gathering.

This is all covered in the work *Scriptures of the Last Days* which is somewhat difficult to find, but ask around and a copy will miraculously come to you. The Lord wants this in the hands of his righteous remnant so they will know these things. This book will soon be republished also so please watch for it. This work contains a complete commentary on Isaiah, Revelation and Daniel citing other relevant scriptures from the standard works.

The question that should be in your mind at this moment is this: What do I have to do to qualify for the exodus? Above, the prophet listed some things which are indicative of the major sins of Ephraim at the moment: the love of things, greed and other forms of idolatry, injustice and dishonesty, and Sabbath breaking. Any additional problems we may have personally need to be corrected as well. There is one other thing which will separate the righteous into two groups; the one who goes on the exodus and the one who stays. The Savior gave a parable about this which is universally misinterpreted in the church. When he had finished talking about the events leading up to his coming, he said that the kingdom at that time would be like a situation he describes:

> *Then shall the kingdom of heaven be likened unto ten virgins, which took their lamps, and went forth to meet the bridegroom. And five of them were wise, and five were foolish. They that were foolish took their lamps, and took no oil with them: But the wise took oil in their vessels with their lamps. While the bridegroom tarried, they all slumbered and slept. And at midnight there was a cry made, Behold, the bridegroom cometh; go ye out to meet him. Then all those virgins arose and trimmed their lamps. And the foolish said unto the wise, Give us of your oil; for our lamps are gone out. But the wise answered, saying, Not so; lest there be not enough for us and you: but go ye rather to them that sell, and buy for yourselves. And while they went to buy, the bridegroom came; and they that were ready went in with him to the marriage: and the door was shut. Afterward came also the other virgins, saying, Lord, Lord, open to us. But he answered and said, Verily I say unto you, I know you not. Watch therefore, for ye know neither the day nor the hour wherein the Son of man cometh.* (Mat 25:1-13)

The Savior is talking about the last days and this is a continuation of his message. The KJV translators put a new chapter here but it is obvious that it does not belong here because of the use of the relative adverb "then." Then, or at that specific time, this situation would arise. If we analyze it carefully, it should be obvious what it means and that our usual explanation is incorrect.

The participants are ten virgins. There have been various ideas who the virgins are but the most common is that they are the members of the church. Unfortunately, in the manner of prophesying of the Jewish prophets, virgin means something else. It means pure, righteous or holy. Since all ten are virgins, or righteous, then it can not very well be all the members of the church, unless by some stretch we can assume the half are pure and holy when only 15 percent qualify for temple recommends. The use of ten by the Lord means a tithe, or a tenth. There are other scriptures (see Isaiah 6:13) which talk about the righteous being a tenth of the people. So what we have are about 10 percent of the members who are pure and righteous.

This does not mean that the 10 percent, or the righteous virgins are taken from the 15 percent who are temple recommend holders. In the temple interview, there is no question which asks if the candidate is an idolater and since this is major sin of Ephraim and general among the church population, it is obvious that many idolaters have recommends and there are many righteous who do not have recommends. But this is judgmental and I have no idea who is righteous and who is not. But the 10 virgins are a tenth of the members and if there are 10 million members now, it amounts to 1 million.

We see something happening that has not happened before. The wedding feast of the Lord is about to take place and the virgins go out to meet him in the figurative sense. But he is not there and has tarried, as the parable says, so the virgins fall asleep. At midnight, the end of the day, they hear the noise of the marriage party. When they hear the party approaching they turn their lamps up but five of the virgins have run out of oil and beg some of the other five who refuse to give them any and tell them to go to the store and buy more.

What is it that the wise virgins have that the foolish ones have run out of? To make sense the oil must represent some commodity. It has always been taught that the oil was faith which is an abstraction and which obviously cannot be shared. But the fact that they ask to share the oil indicates that the oil is something tangible that could be shared if the parties were willing. And since all ten are virgins, or righteous, they all presumably have faith. In order for the metaphor to make sense, as all scriptural metaphors do when interpreted correctly, the oil must not only be something that can be shared, but it must be something which is only significant in this singular circumstance. The oil in this parable is food, specifically the year supply of food. This is the ticket into the wedding feast.

As we look at all parts of the metaphor again it becomes clear. The virgins are all righteous but half of them do not have their year supply of food. They were not prepared with this commodity at the time it was needed.

During the 1960s and early 1970s there was much excitement among the members to prepare the year supply of food and other necessary items. A multitude of food storage suppliers sprang up. There were companies making wheat grinders and people researched ways to store wheat and powdered milk safely. The dehydrated food companies also started manufacturing their products and sold tens of thousands of food storage units. In those years the *Improvement Era*, which was the forerunner of the *Ensign*, was filled with advertisements for every imaginable product or tool for home storage. There were workshops and classes held in the wards and stakes and many talks were given on the subject. Members spent hours at the ward house canning wheat and other things. There were committees appointed to find the commodities to store. There was no end to our labors to comply with this important commandment.

It was generally thought that the second coming was very near. We were in the cold war and expecting a hot war with the USSR at any time. We had just finished WWII and the Korean War and were in the Vietnam War. There was constant war and this was seen as the "wars and rumors of wars" prelude to the tribulation. The leaders of the stakes and wards were very patriotic and basically conservative people who had fought in these wars. The hippie generation had not yet taken over the country and to some extent the church as they have now done. But by the mid-to-late 1970s the fervor had started to die down. Since the signs of his coming, especially the invasion and war with the USSR did not happen, everyone relaxed somewhat. This was the falling asleep of the virgins.

The mid 1970s was the time of President Kimball whose motto

"lengthen our stride" was manifest in an accelerated missionary program and temple building effort. This became the emphasis and not much was said about the food storage program. The nights at the ward ended and those of us who had garages and basements filled with cans of wheat began to ignore it and shuffle it around as necessary.

That is the position we are in today. We are in the part of the parable where we, those of us who are the virgins, are asleep. In 1978-79, at the end of the period of heavy food storage activity, the church made a survey of the wards and stakes to assess the state of our food storage. H. Burke Peterson reported in General Conference in 1979 that about three percent had a year supply of food, about 30 percent had a two or three month supply and the rest had virtually nothing. So after all the frenzy of about 15 years, only three percent wound up with a year supply. When the publicity stopped, people put this important duty on the back burner and that is where we are today. The parable is awaiting fulfillment.

When the noise of the approaching wedding party is heard, or when the tribulation comes, food will be in short supply. Refer to chapter one where the civil war and unrest was discussed. It will revolve around food which will be in short supply. In addition, when the beast takes over, no one will be able to buy or sell unless he takes the mark of the beast. The foolish virgins will find themselves unprepared having procrastinated this most important commandment. They will beg food of their neighbors who were wise enough to prepare but with the food shortage and even famine in some places, those with food will not share and put their own families in danger of starvation.

The wedding begins with the exodus and the birth of Zion which happens in one day. Those who have been righteous and have complied with this one commandment, which has not received much attention lately, will have proven themselves worthy. The year supply of food is the final test of faith. The foolish will have to remain with the rest of the church members and suffer the tribulation that they could have avoided very easily. This is what John means when he says the beast makes war with the remnant of her children who keep the commandments (Rev 12:17). Many others who have been lax in their faithfulness will repent and once again become righteous.

One might say that in this case, we will have to take the mark of the beast to get food. That is correct but taking the mark of the beast is more than an identification. To take the mark requires one to deny Christ and worship the beast, thereby losing one's eternal life. The other option is to see your family go hungry and possibly starve. The paradox here is that those who have their year supply and are otherwise righteous, will not need it because they will be taken by the angels on the exodus shortly after the tribulation starts. Those who do not have it will need it. Maybe it will balance out; when the wise leave on the exodus the foolish can confiscate their food.

This important commandment will be the test. President Benson said in a famous and oft repeated quote that having our year supply of food will be as important as entering the ark in Noah's day. The difference is life or death.

If the same numbers hold true today as in 1979, about three percent of the people have their year supply. The other two percent will be those who have not their food supply because they were unable, such as the very poor, some foreign saints who are unable to do it, and others such as widows and fatherless all of whom would have complied had they the means. This will make the number of people on the exodus about a half million. These are the righteous who form the nation of Zion born in a single day (Isaiah 66:8).

Zion comes into being at this time and the rest of the church does not even know about it. Ninety-five percent of the members will remain and have to go through the tribulation or captivity to purge them of their idolatry and other sins, and unfortunately, many will die. When the captivity is over, those who survive will also then be gathered to Zion by the Davidic prophet who will collect the remainder of scattered Israel from all parts of the world. The object, of course, is to make sure we are on the exodus.

So that is the modern exodus. It is the most important act to occur in this dispensation and it is not even talked about since no one has known about it because Isaiah has been sealed and the Book of Revelation was not understood. It is now unsealed but there is very little time.

If this book did nothing more than explain the woman metaphor of Revelation 12 and the Parable of the Ten Virgins, it would be well worth the price because this information is really priceless and is vitally needed by the righteous members who may not be prepared. There is still time to repent.

Much information has been crammed into this relatively small chapter. We have explained the period of the tribulation and the three major events of this period: the rise of the king of Assyria or the beast, the rise and mission of the Davidic prophet and the exodus. These three events contain most of the minor signs of the last days that people usually dwell on without understanding the major events themselves. Nephi said that men would understand these things at the time they were to be fulfilled (2 Nephi 25:7) so no one is to blame that we did not know them earlier. As you reread these explanations and then read Isaiah (the Gileadi translation) these truths will be evident and they will seem so clear that you will wonder why you did not understand them before. Read these things prayerfully and the Lord will manifest the truth to you at this time.

Chapter III

Act II Midterm Events

As shown on the last days chart, we are now at the midpoint of the last seven years, the point marked 3-1/2 on the time line at the top. There are some events which occur between or during the closing of the sixth seal and opening of the seventh seal. I call them midterm events.

Other writers have written about these events, except for 2 and 3, so they are not unfamiliar, but there may be some additional information given in the following sections. These events are:

- The council at Adam-ondi-Ahman
- The coronation of the Davidic king
- Last days battle of David and Goliath
- Descent of New Jerusalem
- Return of the Ten Tribes
- Sealing of the 144,000

The Great Council at Adam-ondi-Ahman

We do not have much information about the council at Adam-ondi-Ahman except for a couple of scriptures and the statement by Joseph Smith wherein the Lord revealed to him the place, including the name, where the council would be held. But there are a few other scattered references that give us some understanding and much is revealed in Isaiah. Much opinion was given in discourses by early church leaders such as Orson Pratt who may have gotten much of what he says from the prophet Joseph. Most of what they have said on the subject is probably true but there are no scriptures to back up most of it and most of it is unfortunately only opinion. In one particular, most are very much in error as we shall see.

The great council will be held at a place which was then called Spring Hill in Daviess County, Missouri about 75 miles north of Independence.

The item importance for us at this moment is the time of the council since we are principally looking at the major events and their time line. Daniel gives us the time relationships and talks about this council. Daniel is describing the fourth beast or the archtyrant. He sees the 10 horns and the little horn, the antichrist, who comes up among them. The horns are thrones or kings of Europe and the little horn, as we saw, is the king of Assyria or Russia (Dan 7:7-8). Daniel then goes on:

> *I beheld till the thrones were cast down, and the Ancient of days did sit, whose garment was white as snow, and the hair of his head like the pure wool: his throne was like the fiery flame, and his wheels as burning fire. A fiery stream issued and came forth from before him: thousand thousands ministered unto him, and ten thousand times ten thousand stood before him: the judgment was set, and the books were opened. I beheld then because of the voice of the great words which the horn spake: I beheld even till the beast was slain, and his body destroyed, and given to the burning flame.* (Dan 7:9-11)

This is all a single vision presented to Daniel. The thrones were cast down at the time the Ancient of days sits. Since we know from John, "...and power was given unto him to continue forty and two months." (Rev 13:5), this council is being held 42 months after the beast comes to power. See the last days chart where this is shown at the center.

We covered the seventy weeks of Daniel 9 wherein the Davidic king was in Old Jerusalem for most of this time. At the end, he confirmed the covenant with those who had repented and accepted the Savior, then he was rejected and left. When he leaves, the beast is able to overrun the sanctuary which was rebuilt during the seventy weeks. Daniel explains more:

> *And arms shall stand on his part, and they shall pollute the sanctuary of strength, and shall take away the daily sacrifice, and they shall place the abomination that maketh desolate. And such as do wickedly against the covenant shall he corrupt by flatteries: but the people that do know their God shall be strong, and do exploits. And they that understand among the people shall instruct many:...*(Dan 11:31-33)

So he, the archtyrant does away with the daily sacrifice which occurs after week 62 because that is when the Davidic king leaves

Jerusalem. This is a time check also. Later, the angel tells Daniel that the end will be 1290 days from the time the sacrifice is done away. So these are important scriptures for that purpose. It will be in or near the land of Zion that he is destroyed as we mentioned:

> *He shall stretch forth his hand also upon the countries: and the land of Egypt shall not escape. But he shall have power over the treasures of gold and of silver, and over all the precious things of Egypt:...And he shall plant the tabernacles of his palace between the seas in the glorious holy mountain; yet he shall come to his end, and none shall help him.* (Dan 11:42-43, 45)

Some of this was discussed earlier but here we see the time of these events. He invades Egypt, which is the United States, and takes the gold and all other precious things. He sets up his palace here in the "glorious holy mountain" which is Zion or the land of Zion. The holy people of the exodus are there at Adam-ondi-Ahman, the council is in session and the Davidic king is empowered. In a most succinct statement, Daniel says, "he shall come to his end,..." This accurately pins the time down to the end of the sixth seal, 42 months after the beast comes to power.

While we know when the council takes place, little is known of exactly what will take place outside of a couple of general statements such as "the books will be opened" "judgment will sit," and the statements in Daniel and Isaiah concerning the destruction of the king of Assyria. The latter is not really part of the council.

There are many opinions about what will happen and apart from what we are given in a few scriptures, we really have no other information. We know that the 144,000 will be sealed at this time and assigned their last days mission, but it is not clear if it will take place at this council. It is likely that it will, however. There are some things that happen that we do know about, however.

Coronation of the Davidic King

There is one important event which takes place at the great council that is recorded in scripture; the coronation of Israel's king. The only scripture that pertains to this event is found in Daniel:

> *I beheld till the thrones were cast down, and the Ancient of days did sit,...As concerning the rest of the beasts, they had their dominion taken away: yet their lives were pro-*

longed for a season and time. I saw in the night visions, and, behold, one like the Son of man came with the clouds of heaven, and came to the Ancient of days, and they brought him near before him. And there was given him dominion, and glory, and a kingdom, that all people, nations, and languages, should serve him: his dominion is an everlasting dominion, which shall not pass away, and his kingdom that which shall not be destroyed. (Dan 7:9, 12-14)

Verse 9 was quoted earlier. The thrones of the beast and the other countries, especially the three powerful beasts representing England, Germany and Russia, are cast down although the countries and their people apparently remain.

In the midst of discussing these beasts, Daniel sees the event in verses 13 and 14. He sees "one like the Son of man." Every time this phrase is used it is assumed that it refers to the Savior. A close look at the verses in context shows that this cannot be. Nowhere in this chapter does it mention giving dominion to the Savior. It says that dominion is given to the people, specifically to the saints.

Until the Ancient of days came, and judgment was given to the saints of the most High; and the time came that the saints possessed the kingdom. (Dan 7:22)

And the kingdom and dominion, and the greatness of the kingdom under the whole heaven, shall be given to the people of the saints of the most High,... (Dan 7:27)

As we discussed in the previous chapter, this is the reconstituted kingdom of Israel which was to be set up in the last days to never more be ended. This is the kingdom of the Lord's people, the saints. The throne would be occupied by a king of the royal Davidic line, but not the Savior. The time of his legitimate temporal rule over Israel has passed. The royal line has continued and it will belong to the one who is worthy and present. This we know is John. But looking at this scripture further it says that the one like the son of man is brought before Adam.

The idea of the Savior not only coming, but being brought before Adam to receive his kingdom is unreasonable. The Savior after his resurrection said that he received all the glory of his father and became the very father as well as the son. He is the very eternal God, Jehovah in his glorified state, having passed through mortality and is the eternal father having all the power and glory of the father. The one John sees coming is not the Savior.

He is, however, the one mighty and strong, the translated being who has the fulness of the priesthood, the destroyer of the great antichrist, even the Davidic prophet, John the beloved apostle. It is he who is brought before the great first father to receive his dominion. The one who stands before the throne of the Ancient of days is inferior to him. Look at the descriptions of their coming. The Ancient of days comes and is described as a god, which he is. His hair is white as snow and as pure wool, his throne like fiery flame with wheels like burning fire. In addition a fiery stream comes forth before him and thousands minister to him. But when the other comes, he is merely like the Son of man and comes in the clouds of heaven.

The difference in rhetorical description shows that they are superior and inferior respectively. The only way the Savior could be in an inferior relationship is if Adam is God the Father. This is a possibility, although almost no one in the church today believes the Adam/God doctrine. Brigham Young taught that Adam was God and he did so for 18 years and many accepted the doctrine. Brigham said that this was taught by Joseph Smith in private and that some day we would see the truth of it. This is one of the mysteries yet to be revealed. At the present, we have no revelation or scripture on the matter except the ones cited. In these verses he is called the Ancient of days which is defined by Joseph Smith and others as Adam so I must assume for the time being, that it is Adam and not God the Father.

The person receiving the kingdom is the Davidic king now crowned as the king of Israel who will occupy the throne of David until he is replaced, or maybe he will reign forever. The kingdom will, however, last forever and ever. All other political subdivisions which may exist at the time and in the future, will be under his dominion as well; "...and all dominions shall serve and obey him." (Dan 7:27).

The Battle of David and Goliath

This event is not billed this way in the scriptures but it is a reenactment of that famous biblical miracle found in 1 Samuel 17. In the early battle nearly three millennia in the past, the Philistines were battling with Israel and they taunted the armies of Saul with a champion, Goliath. This champion is a type of the last days king of Assyria. Goliath was a giant and no man dared to go to battle against him. He was armed with the best weapons and armor available at that time. He seemed to be invincible.

David was a young man who had firm faith in the God of Israel and was offended when the giant insulted not only the men of Israel but their God as well. In his righteous indignation he offered to go up against the giant.

He refused the king's armor and went against the giant with only his sling with which he either killed or stunned the giant and then took Goliath's sword and cut off his head. The army of Saul then pursued the Philistines and won the victory.

We have read the scriptures in Daniel talking about the destruction of the king of Assyria, or the beast as he calls him. Isaiah also describes the events:

> *You will take up this taunt against the king of Babylon, and say, How the tyrant has met his end and tyranny ceased! The Lord has broken the staff of the wicked, the rod of those who ruled, him who with unerring blows struck down the nations in anger, who subdued peoples in his wrath by relentless oppression. Now the whole earth is at rest and at peace;...All rulers of nations lie in state, each among his own kindred. But you are cast away unburied like a repugnant fetus, exposed like the slain disfigured by the sword, whose mangled remains are thrown in a gravel pit. You shall not share burial with them, for you have destroyed your land and murdered your people. May the brood of miscreants never more be mentioned! Prepare for the massacre of their sons, in consequence of their fathers' deeds, lest they rise up again and take possession of the world, and fill the face of the earth with cities. I will rise up against them, says the Lord of Hosts. I will cut off Babylon's name and remnant, its offspring and descendants, says the Lord. The Lord of Hosts made an oath, saying, As I foresaw it, so shall it happen; as I planned it, so shall it be: I will break Assyria in my own land, trample them underfoot on my mountains; their yoke shall be taken from them, their burden removed from their*

> *shoulders. These are things determined upon the whole earth; this is the hand upraised over all nations. For what the Lord of Hosts has determined, who shall revoke? When his hand is upraised, who can turn it away?* (Isaiah 14:4-7, 18-27)

This is quite a long quote but the whole chapter deals with the death of the king of Assyria. It is very amusing in some parts. We are told several things. First the tyrant, like Goliath, is left unburied. The Lord gives an especially graphic description of this particular curse. One of the covenant curses of an unrighteous king in ancient suzerain/vassal relationships was to be unburied. As an unrighteous king, he suffers this curse as did King Ahab who, with his pagan wife Jezebel, led Israel into pagan idolatry, and who was left unburied for dogs to rend and devour.

A second covenant curse is to be deprived of offspring. When people read of the killing of the children of kings they are horrified at the cruelty of the people of those times. But here the Lord is saying the same thing.

When Zedekiah was captured after breaking his covenant with the king of Babylon, he witnessed the slaughter of his children before his eyes and then he was blinded. This is done to prevent any vengeance by the offspring and to cut off the lineage of an unrighteous king. The Lord states the same thing here. In verse 21, the Lord decrees "the massacre of their sons" so they will not rise up and possess the world again. One of the great covenant blessings of Lord is to have eternal offspring and numerous progeny. But the Lord says he will cut off their name so completely that it will not be remembered nor spoken.

As quoted in the last chapter and above in this chapter, the Lord will break the king of Assyria and his followers in this land, or on his mountains. Mountains are both literal and metaphorical. Before he said that they would be destroyed in his holy mountain. Here mountains is plural indicating that he is speaking in both the literal and metaphorical modes. They will be broken in the nation of Zion and upon the mountains of this land.

Finally, the Lord tells us who will do the deed. In the last two verses he says "this is the hand upraised over all nations" and When his hand is upraised, who can turn it away?" The hand, as we learned in the last chapter, is the Davidic king and it is he who will destroy the king of Assyria. In the previous chapter we cited many scriptures indicating that the Davidic king would free the captives and break the yoke of bondage. We will not requote them here.

The Davidic king will not be armed with conventional weapons as he goes to battle with the king of Assyria. The beast is armed with the most state-of-the-art weapons of our time. With these weapons he has conquered the entire world. Against this armed might, the Davidic king seems to be the underdog but he will destroy the king of Assyria just as his predecessor and namesake killed Goliath with a small, white, round stone. The stone is symbolic of the Davidic king also because he is foretold as a stone being placed in Zion and we examined that in detail.

> *The Lord will cause his voice to resound, and make visible his arm descending in furious rage, with flashes of devouring fire, explosive discharges and pounding hail. At the voice of the Lord the Assyrians will be terror-stricken, they who used to strike with the rod. At every sweep of the staff of authority, when the Lord lowers it upon them, they will be fought in mortal combat.* (Isaiah 30:30-32)

"Voice" and "arm" are the Davidic king. The Lord now sends his voice and lowers his arm in rage on the Assyrians. The Davidic king uses the elements and sends "devouring fire, explosive discharges and pounding hail" on the Assyrians. And like the Philistines, they will be terror stricken. How can they hope to fight against these weapons? The Philistines fled in terror when they saw their champion felled by a boy. In this way the Assyrians will be mostly destroyed.

> *And Assyria shall fall by a sword not of man; a sword not of mortals shall devour them: before that sword they shall waste away and their young men melt; Their captain shall expire in terror and their officers shrink from the ensign, says the Lord, whose fire is in Zion, whose furnace is in Jerusalem.* (Isaiah 31:8-9)

Here the Lord calls the Davidic king by several of his metaphorical names. This is why it is important to understand the use of symbols and metaphor without which it is impossible to understand this most important of prophetic books. This is why his people could not understand it, said Nephi.

The sword is the Davidic king. He is the sword in the mouth of the Lord in Revelation:

And I saw heaven opened, and behold a white horse; and he that sat upon him was called Faithful and True, and in righteousness he doth judge and make war. His eyes were as a flame of fire, and on his head were many crowns; and he had a name written, that no man knew, but he himself. And he was clothed with a vesture dipped in blood: and his name is called the Word of God. And the armies which were in heaven followed him upon white horses, clothed in fine linen, white and clean. And out of his mouth goeth a sharp sword, that with it he should smite the nations: and he shall rule them with a rod of iron: and he treadeth the winepress of the fierceness and wrath of Almighty God. And he hath on his vesture and on his thigh a name written, KING OF KINGS AND LORD OF LORDS. (Rev 19:11-16)

This whole quote is a metaphorical and symbolic presentation of the Savior in his last-day's role as the judge who brings justice and salvation to the world. There are several items of affirmation which show this to be the Lord and no one will make a mistake here. He is the Word, or Logos, which is one of his names. He is dressed in red which is the way he will appear. He has many crowns on his head and he is identified as the King of Kings and Lord of Lords which is a title of the Savior only.

The sword coming out of his mouth, however, is the Davidic king. This was mentioned elsewhere, especially in Isaiah. We quoted Isaiah 49:2 where the Davidic prophet speaks. In these verses the Davidic prophet said he was called before he was in the womb, etc. In verse 2 he says, "He has made my mouth like a sharp sword—in the shadow of his hand he hid me. He has made me into a polished arrow—in his quiver he kept me secret." From this we understand that he will be a warrior king as was David of old. He will be the sword and the arrow to destroy the Lord's enemies, the Philistines, in the last days. Another scripture where the Lord refers to him as his sword is Isaiah 34:

When my sword drinks its fill in the heavens, it shall come down on Edom in judgment, on the people I have sentenced to damnation. The Lord has a sword that shall en-

gorge with blood and glut itself with fat—the blood of lambs and he-goats, the kidney fat of rams. For the Lord will hold a slaughter in Bozrah, an immense massacre in the land of Edom; (Isaiah 34:5-6)

The Davidic king was taken to heaven in the metaphor in Revelation 12. During the nearly two millennia John has been on the earth, he has been preparing for his great mission and when he is prepared and the time comes, he will come down on the earth as the Lord's sword. The terms Edom and Bozrah are types of the land and cities of the gentile world.

In that day will the Lord, with his great and powerful sword, punish severely Leviathan, the evasive maritime serpent, Leviathan, that devious sea monster, when he slays the dragons of the Sea. (Isaiah 27:1)

The navies of the king of Assyria will not be safe. The Lord's "great and powerful sword," who is the Davidic king again, will destroy the ships and submarines who are the dragons of the sea. But this is metaphorical as well. Water and seas are people. The people of the antichrist are very numerous consisting of the vast population of the USSR and China. The dragons of the sea are also the leaders of the armies in the symbolic sense.

See, the Lord comes with fire, his chariots like a whirlwind, to retaliate in furious anger, to rebuke with conflagrations of fire. For with fire and with his sword shall the Lord execute judgment on all flesh, and those slain by the Lord shall be many. (Isaiah 66:15-16)

This is another example of the use of "sword" to refer to the Davidic king. The various verses are somewhat repetitive but the Lord repeats things, especially his warnings, so that we will pay attention and remember.

The sons of Ephraim and those with them will perform the mop-up operation.

Your sons shall hasten your ravagers away—those who ruined you shall depart from you. (Isaiah 49:17)

As in the days of the first David, the armies of Israel pursued the Philistines and finished the job of defeating them. They will find no safety. The vast armies of the Russians, Chinese and other allies will be wiped out by the great power they have.

Those who have been on the exodus, as we discovered, will

be translated beings and will have much the same power as the Davidic king himself and will operate under his direction just as he operates under direction of the Savior.

The New Jerusalem

Since the early days of the church, there has been great interest in the establishment of New Jerusalem on this continent in Jackson County. It was revealed to Joseph Smith that there would be a temple built there and the temple lot was dedicated. The Saints were commanded to buy property for their inheritance. For this reason they anticipated that the establishment would be very soon; in their lifetimes. We have very little information on this except again from early talks found in the *Journal of Discourses* and other records. Most of the information is opinion and speculation, even though they were general authorities.

The most common myth is that one day a large group of people will be called and assembled to go back and begin the building of that city. Joseph F. Smith described his idea of a band of about 300,000 wending their way to Jackson County with cattle and wagons, defending themselves against enemies who were attacking from all sides. (JD 24:156-57).

We have described the exodus in detail from the scriptures and the picture is very different from President Smith's description. There will be no cattle and no enemies along the way. The people will be taken by angels into the wilderness without taking anything with them. They will be fed along the way for two years and there will be no enemies to harass them except for the initial army the beast sends to pursue them.

This group of the righteous remnant will not be called by the First Presidency or by anyone. They will just disappear.

> *The righteous disappear, and no man gives it a thought; the godly are gathered out, but no one perceives that from impending calamity the righteous are withdrawn.* (Isaiah 57:1)

This is because they are taken by angels in an instant. An undertaking such as President Smith depicts would take months in the planning. The truth is very different as we now know.

The Saints on the exodus will be in the wilderness during most of the tribulation period when the king of Assyria is rampaging and conquering the world. When the Saints on the exodus reach the land of Zion, the former inhabitants will have been wiped out by the king of Assyria. He will have set up his palace and his tabernacles there.

This is Satan's doing. He will try to occupy and secure the land since he knows very well where it is located. This is why the great council at Adam-ondi-Ahman will not be held in New Jerusalem proper. At the council, the judgment will be made to remove the king of Assyria since he has completed his role as the Lord's scourge. The first 3-1/2 years are over and he must end. So the Davidic king and the sons of Ephraim will destroy the king of Assyria and drive his armies out and or destroy them. This is the redemption of Zion or the land of Zion by power. (D&C 103:15).

When the land is cleared of the Assyrians, the part of the city which is in heaven will descend:

> *And I John saw the holy city, new Jerusalem, coming down from God out of heaven, prepared as a bride adorned for her husband. And I heard a great voice out of heaven saying, Behold, the tabernacle of God is with men, and he will dwell with them, and they shall be his people, and God himself shall be with them, and be their God. And there came unto me one of the seven angels...and talked with me saying, Come hither, I will shew thee the bride, the Lamb's wife. And he carried me away in the spirit to a great and high mountain, and shewed me that great city, the holy Jerusalem, descending out of heaven from God.* (Rev 21:2-3, 9-10)

John was privileged to see New Jerusalem coming down from heaven. This is a prefabricated, ready to go city with no need of electricity nor other utilities. The water will flow out of it.

Just how much building there will be to do is not mentioned except that the people who come may have to build houses. The temple at Independence will have to be built, presumably, but even that could be transported down because there is talk of the Lord's temple in heaven which is in the midst of the New Jerusalem.

> *And they that have been scattered shall be gathered. Zion shall not be moved out of her place, notwithstanding her children are scattered. They that remain, and are pure in*

heart, shall return, and come to their inheritances, they and their children, with songs of everlasting joy, to build up the waste places of Zion. (D&C 101:13, 17-18)

As the people are gathered during the next few months, they will build up the waste places; the areas where the great destruction took place. They will clean the homes and move into them. Isaiah talks about the people inhabiting the vacant houses.

Because of them the fortified cities lie forlorn, deserted habitations, forsaken like a wilderness;... (Isaiah 27:10)

This is talking about the cities of the United States. "Them" in this verse refers to the fiery blasts and east wind. This is another reference to the Davidic king who is the east wind and he delivers the fiery blasts that destroy the Assyrians but not the cities. So the building up will consist of mostly cleanup and there will not likely be much heavy construction going on.

The people who arrive from the exodus and the people of Enoch and whoever else may descend, will be translated beings with powers pertaining to the terrestrial order. These people can transport themselves without mechanical means and are impervious to injury. They will not be required to do work in the way it is now done in our telestial order. The establishment of New Jerusalem will proceed very quickly.

In the *Dead Sea Scrolls*, there is a work called "The New Jerusalem (5Q15)." The fragment contains a description of the city in some detail. The writer of the book was accompanying an angel acting as a surveyor who measured everything from the size of the blocks of houses, the avenues and the streets, to the detailed dimensions of rooms, stairs and windows. The fragment in cave 5 is only part of the book and another fragment, unpublished yet, was found in cave 4. Other fragments of this book were found in caves 1, 2 and 11. When they are all translated and published, there should be quite a complete description. (There are several books which contain excerpts and full reproductions of the translated fragments collected into fascicles. Among them are commentaries on Isaiah. The official fascicles are published in separate works and are quite expensive. Fascicles 1-3 are about $140 and Fascicle 4, which is just published costs about $65 if you are serious about them.)

The interesting thing about this scroll is that it is almost identical to the experience John recorded in Revelation 11:1-2 where he is given a reed or measuring rod and told to measure the temple. This is the temple in Old Jerusalem which will be rebuilt in the 70 weeks under the direction of John. In the New Jerusalem scroll, the person doing the measuring is an angel, and is John whose mission in part, is to direct the building.

The establishment of New Jerusalem will be almost an instantaneous event and will not require months or years of building. It will happen and be established in the interregnum period or the space between the first 42 months of the tribulation and the 42 months of the judgment period which come back-to-back. The midterm events described herein will have to take place in a very brief period at the end of the first period and beginning of the second period. All of the events in this chapter could take place in two or three weeks.

When the king of Assyria is destroyed, as we read above, there will be a period of peace. People will be relieved to be free from the bondage of this tyrant. It will be much like the period following World War II when the Axis powers were destroyed. There was a period of peace and rejoicing throughout the world. There was no war nor contention for a time. People were trying to find lost loved ones who had disappeared during the war. It was a bittersweet time, but it did not last long. In less than a year following the war, there was warfare in the Middle East and as the years have passed, there have been continual wars somewhere on the globe.

This short period of peace will see people returning to their own native lands. "Then, like a deer that is chased, or a flock of sheep that no one rounds up, each will return to his own people and everyone flee to his own homeland." (Isaiah 13:14). The captives that were freed will return home. There is a hint here from the context that the people will flee home because there are beginning to be some natural disturbances which characterize the judgment period discussed in the next chapter. At any rate, this short period of quiet allows people to try to return to a more nearly normal existence once again.

Return of the Ten Tribes

The Ten Tribes cannot return until the king of Assyria is destroyed, therefore, the coming has to be in the interregnum period. They have to come after the Council at Adam-ondi-Ahman because they are part of the gathering which is a post-council event. The great council is composed of very high-level people from the various dispensations and we, the ordinary people, with the exception of the people on the exodus, will not participate. The exact order of appearance of the Ten Tribes is not known except that leading them back is one of the duties of the Davidic king. He is their king as well.

> *He will raise the ensign to the nations and assemble the exiled of Israel; he will gather the scattered of Judah from the four directions of the earth. The Lord will dry up the tongue of the Egyptian Sea by his mighty wind; he will extend his hand over the River and smite it into seven streams, to provide a way on foot. And there shall be a pathway out of Assyria for the remnant of his people who shall be left, as there was for Israel when it came up from the land of Egypt.* (Isaiah 11:12, 15-16)

The ensign is not the church here as some argue, but in Isaiah is a metaphor for the Davidic king, although the church has been gathering as many of Israel as possible. The prophecies in Isaiah pertain to the last seven years of this dispensation, however, and only to the events of that period. He will also gather the scattered of Judah.

Mighty wind is another metaphor for the Davidic king. He was called the "east wind" earlier (Isaiah 27:8). The tongue of the Egyptian Sea will be dried up. As we learned before, water is people and the tongue refers to the people of the eastern part of the United States. The prophecies of Brigham Young and Heber C. Kimball have been read many times attesting to the fact that the eastern part of the United States will be deserted. I will not quote them here because they are familiar to most.

"River" is capitalized indicating that it is a proper name. The Lord referred to the king of Assyria as a mighty river which overflows its banks. A river is an army and here again is the hand of the Lord, the Davidic king, extended over the river and it is divided into seven streams to provide a way on foot. In other words, the army of the beast is shattered and scattered allowing people to travel between them.

While this is going on, a pathway is established from Assyria, which is Russia, for those of Israel in that country to come to Zion. If the Ten Tribes are in the north of Russia or Siberia as many believe, this could refer to them. In any case, the highway is for the return of Israel from that land. The very idea of a highway, or pathway, suggests the movement of a lot of people. He said:

> *It is too small a thing for you to be my servant to raise up the tribes of Jacob and to restore those preserved of Israel. I will also appoint you to be a light to the nations,...* (Isaiah 49:5-6)

The job of restoring the tribes of Israel is given to the Davidic prophet, who is also the prophet of the Ten Tribes. Joseph Smith said in 1831, that John was at that time among the Ten Tribes. John Whitmer recorded the events of the church conference held June 3-6, 1831:

> *The Spirit of the Lord fell upon Joseph in an unusual manner, and he prophesied that John the Revelator was then among the Ten Tribes of Israel who had been led away by Shalmanesser, king of Assyria, to prepare them for their return from their long dispersion, to again possess the land of their fathers.* (DHC 1:176)

So John, the Davidic prophet/king was even then ministering among his people. He was, then, their prophet. The modern revelation that mentions their coming is found in Doctrine and Covenants:

> *And they who are in the north countries shall come in remembrance before the Lord; and their prophets shall hear his voice, and shall no longer stay themselves; and they shall smite the rocks, and the ice shall flow down at their presence.* (D&C 133:26)

This revelation will be discussed in more detail in the next section in conjunction with the sealing of the 144,000. But this speaks of the coming of the Ten Tribes. They will be led by the Davidic prophet, who is mentioned here by his metaphorical name, "voice." Isaiah mentions the return although his words are not quoted by other commentators on the last days because, again, they have not understood this book.

> *In that day my Lord will again raise his hand to reclaim the remnant of his people—those who shall be left out of Assyria, Egypt, Pathros, Cush, Elam, Shinar, Hamath, and*

the islands of the Sea. He will raise the ensign to the nations and assemble the exiled of Israel;...The Lord will dry up the tongue of the Egyptian Sea by his mighty wind; he will extend his hand over the River and smite it into seven streams, to provide a way on foot. And there shall be a pathway out of Assyria for the remnant of his people who shall be left, as there was for Israel when it came up from the land of Egypt. (Isaiah 11:11-12, 15-16)

Again we see the several metaphors for the Davidic king; the Lord raises his "hand." He raises the "ensign." He dries up the tongue of the Egyptian Seas by his "mighty wind." Earlier we quoted the Lord calling him the "east wind." He will extend his "hand" over the River and smite it into seven streams. We know that the river is the army of the king of Assyria and this indicates that the Davidic king divides them into seven groups so that those who return will be able to pass between them. He also states here as in D&C 133, that there will be a "pathway out of Assyria for the remnant of his people who shall be left." This obviously refers to the Ten Tribes.

In that day the Lord will thresh out his harvest from the torrent of the River to the streams of Egypt. But you shall be gleaned one by one, O children of Israel. In that day a loud trumpet shall sound, and they who were lost in the land of Assyria and they who were outcasts in the land of Egypt shall come and bow down to the Lord in the holy mountain at Jerusalem. (Isaiah 27:12-13)

The Lord again uses a metaphor for the restoration of the exiles, that of threshing. But the people are being gathered out from the torrent of the River, who is still Assyria, to the streams of Egypt, which is the United States. He makes it clear that the ones who are lost, the Ten Tribes, are lost in Assyria, which is Russia. The ones who were outcasts in Egypt are, of course, Ephraim who were driven out of their own country of Egypt and later taken captive again becoming exiles in their own land. The close relationship with, and near worship of this government by the corporate church today belies the real relationship that lasted for several decades. But in the end both Ephraim and the Ten Tribes will bow down in the holy mountain, or nation of Zion at New Jerusalem.

It should be fairly obvious from the scriptures cited here, and there are others, that the Ten Tribes are on this planet, in the north of Asia, or Russia. They will be led back by the Davidic king with power, and it is he who really has the power to smite the rocks, which are people, and the enemy armies.

The Sealing of the 144,000

This is one of the many miraculous events that will be happening during this fantastic period. Wonder after wonder will be presented before those who are privileged to see them and many of the wonders will be terrible. One of the wonderful things to take place is the calling of a special group of missionaries to go into the world during the final 3-1/2 years to gather the scattered of Israel and other righteous souls who desire to come to Zion.

Beyond what I have said in the foregoing paragraph, there has been little known until recently when Isaiah was unsealed. There we see a little more of these men in action but mostly we know from the mission of the Davidic prophet what their duties are. We also gain some understanding of where they come from since there is little given regarding their origin. The only place we read anything about it is in Revelation where John mentions them:

> *And I heard the number of them that were sealed: and there were sealed an hundred and forty and four thousand of all the tribes of the children of Israel. Of the tribe of Judah were sealed twelve thousand....* (Rev 7:4-8)

John gives us the number, which is the only place it is given. He also says that they come from all the children of Israel. He lists the tribes of Israel but conspicuously omits Dan.

At first glance it would appear that John is saying that 12,000 will be chosen from each tribe and most commentators hold this view. This fact would imply that the Ten Tribes would have to return before the sealing, naturally. This creates a paradox because it is the role of the Davidic king and the servants with him, the 144,000, to gather the scattered of Israel, including the Ten Tribes. In fact it is explicit that this is one of their duties. If so, then the selection is not from the Ten Tribes. The Lord has given some information about this to Joseph Smith:

> *And the Lord, even the Savior, shall stand in the midst of his people, and shall reign over all flesh. And they who*

> *are in the north countries shall come in remembrance before the Lord; and their prophets shall hear his voice, and shall no longer stay themselves; and they shall smite the rocks, and the ice shall flow down at their presence. And an highway shall be cast up in the midst of the great deep. Their enemies shall become a prey unto them. And in the barren deserts there shall come forth pools of living water; and the parched ground shall no longer be a thirsty land. And they shall bring forth their rich treasures unto the children of Ephraim, my servants. And the boundaries of the everlasting hills shall tremble at their presence. And there they shall they fall down and be crowned with glory, even in Zion, by the hands of the servants of the Lord, even the children of Ephraim. And they shall be filled with songs of everlasting joy. Behold, this is the blessing of the everlasting God upon the tribes of Israel, and the richer blessing upon the head of Ephraim and his fellows.* (D&C 133:25-34)

These verses, particularly the ones referring to the people coming from the north countries smiting the rocks and the ice flowing down before them, are well known and often quoted. The Lord uses a generous sprinkling of metaphor and symbol which, however, is usually ignored. In this passage we are told of the return of the Ten Tribes who are scattered in the north countries. Just what this means has been conjectured to mean various things.

There are theories that they are on a different planet, that they have been translated and will come with the city of Enoch. President Joseph Fielding Smith suggested that they might be in giant caves underneath the northern ice pack. There is also the hollow-earth theory. I must confess that I do not know where they are except that they are on the earth, this earth, somewhere, and apparently in the north of Asia especially in Russia as we read above. The Lord reiterates that they are in the north countries.

In the last days, after the tribulation, they will be gathered to Zion where they will come singing songs of joy. (This is a metaphor for worship.) The important information in this revelation is that they will come and receive their blessings (endowments, etc.) at the hands of Ephraim. It is Ephraim who holds the keys and has received the commission to gather the lost of Israel and we have been attempting to do that for the past 166 years. We have pretty much gathered Ephraim, or at least identified them and set up stakes where those outside the Utah area live. The other tribes will also be gathered by Ephraim.

But what about the statement in Revelation? I believe that this is a misunderstanding. It is either a mistranslation, something is missing or we are simply reading it wrong because it conflicts with the modern revelation from D&C 133 which we know is a correct rendering. John gives some further light on the matter:

> *And I looked, and lo, a Lamb stood on the mount Sion, and with him an hundred forty and four thousand, having his Father's name written in their foreheads. And I heard a voice from heaven, as the voice of many waters, and as the voice of a great thunder: and I heard the voice of harpers harping with their harps. And they sung as it were a new song before the throne, and before the four beasts, and the elders: and no man could learn that song but the hundred and forty and four thousand, which were redeemed from the earth. These are they which were not defiled with women; for they are virgins. These are they which follow the Lamb whithersoever he goeth. These were redeemed from among men, being the firstfruits unto God and to the Lamb. And in their mouth was found no guile: for they are without fault before the throne of God.* (Rev 14:1-5)

In the last days, the Lord stands on Mount Zion. This as you know by now, is a metaphor for the nation or people of Zion. The Lord stands among the people of Zion which was born in a day at the exodus. He is among them. With the Savior in Zion, are the 144,000 "which were redeemed from the earth." In other words, they were saved from the world by the exodus. For this reason, they are the first fruits. Those who did not make it on the exodus have to wait a while. They have to suffer the captivity of the king of Assyria for a few months, up to 42, and then they too, the ones who are purged of their idolatry and/or repent, will come to Zion.

John gives a little more definition. He states that they are virgins. When I was a young man and a missionary, I thought this meant that they were young men who were not married but were chaste and virginal. It does not mean that. These virgins are the same virgins from the parable who went on the exodus; the wise ones. So the 144,000 are not chosen from the 12 tribes but are the adult males who were on the exodus. This is the only group which will be ready and worthy.

When we discussed the exodus in chapter two, we learned that the people who are on the exodus will be translated and have their call and election made sure by the time the exodus ends. The Savior will be in their midst, as he has promised, and as we cited.

We estimated from the size of the church and the percentage the Lord gives, five percent, that there will be roughly a half million on the exodus. This would make the ratio of young boys over 12 and men, to women and children about 1:2.5 which seems to be about right.

There are a couple of additional time checks in this passage (D&C 133). The Lord says, "and they shall smite the rocks, and the ice shall flow down at their presence. And an highway shall be cast up in the midst of the great deep." We will cover this phenomenon in the next chapter in detail. Remember the verses in Revelation:

> *And I saw another angel ascending from the east, having the seal of the living God: and he cried with a loud voice to the four angels, to whom it was given to hurt the earth and the sea, Saying, Hurt not the earth, neither the sea, nor the trees, till we have sealed the servants of our God in their foreheads. And I heard the number of them which were sealed: and there were sealed an hundred and forty and four thousand....* (Rev 7:2-4)

This angel, as we saw, is the Davidic prophet who tells the angels not to hurt the earth or the sea. The great natural events which John describes in Revelation, occur in the second period of 3-1/2 years. The scorching heat that melts the ice occurs at this time also, and that is when the Ten Tribes return. Notice that John tells the angels not to do this until after the 144,000 are sealed, hence they can not be selected from the Ten Tribes. The seas are dried up during this judgment period as well.

He also says there will be a highway cast up in the sea. The seas are drying up in the searing heat and the Lord has said that dry land will appear where there was sea. Isaiah mentions the highway also:

In that day there shall be a highway from Egypt to Assyria. Assyrians shall come to Egypt and Egyptians go to Assyria, and the Egyptians will labor with the Assyrians. (Isaiah 19:23).

This is after the king of Assyria is destroyed and peace reigns for a little while. Egypt is the United States and Assyria is Russia. It is too much of a coincidence that the highway is specifically between the two places where the Ten Tribes are to pass. As the oceans recede and the land is gathered together once again, this high and dry passageway will exist for the people, but it will be after the 144,000 are sealed and they will guide the Ten Tribes in their own exodus back to Zion to be crowned by Ephraim, or in other words, to receive their endowments. Ephraim will already be there waiting for them in Zion.

D&C 133 says that the barren desert will have pools of water and the parched land will no longer be thirsty. This is metaphor talk. Water is people and the people will be in the desert making their way to Zion. This is not only the Ten Tribes but others will do so as well, although here it is specifically referring to the Ten Tribes.

They will also bring their rich treasure to Zion. This is also metaphorical. Elsewhere, these treasures are referred to as precious vessels. These are the children. I have heard people comment on these verses and remark that the Ten Tribes will bring silver and gold to be used in the building of the temple. They may do so, but that is not what this means. It is very doubtful that the people will have any silver and gold left after the tribulation.

Much of the foregoing information can be derived by reason which also raises some interesting questions. The Ten Tribes were taken into captivity about 725 BC which is over 2700 years ago. Is it possible for a people to exist this long and retain their homogeneity? If they were living as a single group, they would have experienced tremendous growth and would number in the hundreds of millions by now. It would be almost impossible for them to have remained lost under these circumstances unless, as President Smith asserted, they are under the ice in large caves. This begs additional questions. The consensus of most scholars of my acquaintance is that the Ten Tribes are mingled with the people of northern Asia, especially Russian Siberia and that they are not a homogeneous body, but rather, like Ephraim who was mixed with the peoples of northwestern Europe, they are mixed with Asian peoples and thus hidden from the world.

Hosea and Amos, however, give us some information that may explain the mystery. The Lord has ways of doing things that are sometimes simple yet effective. Hosea was talking to the kingdom of Israel or Ephraim as it was called which consisted of the ten tribes.

> *Ephraim—their honor will fly like a bird from [the time of] birth or from the womb or from conception. For if they shall rear their children I will bereave them from manhood, for woe is to them as well when I turn away from them. Ephraim is as I saw Tyre, implanted in [her] dwelling place; but Ephraim [seeks] to take his children out to the slayer. Give to them, Lord, what you will give; give to them a bereaving womb and shriveled breasts…Ephraim has been smitten; their root is withered; they will not produce fruit; even if they gave birth I will slay the treasures of their wombs. My God shall spurn them for they have not obeyed Him and they shall wander among the nations.* (Hosea 9:11-14, 16-17)
>
> *So said the Lord: Just as the shepherd rescues from the mouth of the lion two legs or the cartilage of the ear, so shall be saved from the Children of Israel who dwell in Samaria the corner of a bed and [some] of the cloth of a couch.* (Amos 3:12)
>
> *For so said the Lord God: The city from which go forth a thousand shall leave a hundred, and one from which go forth a hundred shall leave ten to the House of Israel.* (Amos 5:3)
>
> *For, lo, I will command, and I will sift the house of Israel among all nations, like as corn is sifted in a sieve, yet shall not the least grain fall upon the earth. All the sinners of my people shall die by the sword, which say, The evil shall not overtake nor prevent us.* (Amos 9:9-10)

What the Lord is saying in these verses is that the kingdom will be destroyed and most of the people will be destroyed as well. In our classes when we have studied the captivity of Israel, we have conceived of most or all of the people being marched off into captivity. The truth is that from cities of thousands only hundreds were spared to go into captivity. I have not cited the verses here but both Hosea and Amos describe the invaders splitting open the pregnant women and killing them and their babies. All the old and the very young were killed.

Ephraim was the largest tribe and the others were quite small to begin with. So of the nine tribes beside Ephraim, there were probably very few people. Ephraim migrated to northeastern Europe while the other tribes disappeared in Asia. The Lord here gives a further curse to the tribes. He is saying that from this time on, at least during the exile, Ephraim and all of Israel would have very few children. They would only produce sufficient offspring to maintain the lineage. So when the church was restored in 1830 and the gathering of Ephraim began, there were only a few thousand living in northern Europe and England.

The other nine tribes were similarly cursed. While I was studying the peoples and languages of Asia, I came upon the nomadic peoples of the steppes and the Islamic republics. These people are small groups or tribes who have wandered for centuries and no one really knows where they came from. They migrate from the plains in the winter to the higher elevations in the summer. They do not live in cities so the governments of the lands where they lived have pretty much ignored them. They live the same today as they have lived for hundreds or thousands of years. It is very possible that these groups of nomads are the remnants of the nine tribes. They have been cursed with few offspring; only sufficient to maintain their number. The inbreeding probably causes much miscarrying as well.

But these same prophets state that Israel will once more flourish.

> *I will be to Israel like the dew; he shall blossom like the rose, and his roots shall strike out like the Lebanon. His branches shall go forth, and his beauty shall be like [that of] the olive and his fragrance like [that of] the Lebanon. Those who dwell in his shade shall return; they shall revive like the grain and sprout like the wine; its mention [shall be] like the wine of Lebanon.* (Hosea 14:5-7)

These verses are familiar to us. In the last days of the gathering, Ephraim, meaning all of Israel, will blossom and be fruitful once more. We have witnessed this with Ephraim after the gathering and will yet see the other nine tribes grow when they come forth at this time.

The bottom line is that the 144,000 will be sealed in the interregnum period. They will consist of the adult males who were on the exodus. By the time the exodus reaches Zion (Jackson County) they will be translated, have their call and election made sure and will be prepared to go into the world during the final 3-1/2 years of the judgment period to gather the remainder of Israel, including the remaining nine tribes, to Zion.

Chapter IV

Act III The Judgment

While the intermediate events are still taking place and after a short period of peace, the scene changes drastically. The Lord describes the period as being so terrible that there never was such a time in the history of the world nor will there be again. During this short span of 3-1/2 years, the earth will virtually be depopulated. All those who are of a telestial law, which is the majority of people, will have to leave before the Millennium begins.

To get some idea of the magnitude of this destruction we can reduce it to numbers. There are over five billion people on the earth at present. The tribulation period will take a large toll but it will be a drop in the bucket. The Nazis tried to slaughter people as fast as they could but they only succeeded in killing a few million. With the deaths from battle, disease and other causes, the total was about 100 million. This is a fantastic number when we think about it because a million is such a huge number but small compared to the billions who will perish.

Let us assume that there are one billion righteous souls on the earth who are qualified for the terrestrial order. I do not think the number is anywhere near that large, but for this example's sake we can assume this figure. That would leave about four billion people who have to be eliminated. The Lord says that mankind will be scarce. (Isaiah 13:12, 24:6) The judgment will last for 1260 days, which is slightly less than 42 months but if you work it out, you will see that about 3.1 million will have to perish every day during the 42 months in order to eliminate the four billion by the time the judgment period ends. This is an astounding figure and it boggles the mind to contemplate death on such a scale. There will only be two places where it will be safe to reside; Old Jerusalem and New Jerusalem. Old Jerusalem will not be too safe either. The Lord has said that all who will not take up the sword must flee to Zion for safety (D&C 45:68).

The Lord has referred to his marvelous work and a wonder

from Isaiah. Members of the church have thought this referred to the restoration of the gospel and the work of carrying it to the world, but this has nothing to do with the restoration of the church. The marvelous work and wonder he will perform pertains to the great "slaughter in Bozrah" which will take place at this time. We misunderstand the words used. Wonder, for example, meant something awesome or beyond understanding. Today, it has the sense of something that is surprisingly good. Marvelous is the same thing. Formerly it meant mysterious or frightening. Today, it is associated with good. The sense in which the Lord uses it is as something bizarre. In Isaiah, Gileadi translates it a strange work and bizarre.

In Elizabethan times, which is the language of the KJV, words had different shadings and meanings. For example, "awful" today means something bad as when someone feels bad or has an awful experience. When St. Paul's church in London was destroyed and rebuilt by Sir Robert Wren, King Charles looked on the great building and said it was "awful." He also said it was "artificial." A modern architect would have been insulted but what he was really saying was something like our word "awesome." In his day, awful meant something that inspires awe. Artificial today means something faked or phony. But to King Charles it meant something made with great art or craft. The point here is that it is a good idea to have an OED handy when we read the KJV.

This period is the continuation of the great and terrible day of the Lord and it gets more terrible as it progresses. It is so horrible, in fact, that we do not read about these things in our church classes because they turn people off. The descriptions are gruesome in the extreme. But the Lord gave us these scriptures so that we would be horrified and in contemplating the things that are to happen, we might repent and be prepared. In this chapter we will look at the verbal paintings and read explicit details for this same purpose.

There are two important things that will be happening during this period. The first is the slaughter of all of mankind who are not or who do not wish to be among the righteous. The second major event is the gathering of the rest of Israel. This will be accomplished by the Davidic prophet and the 144,000. We will deal with these two sets of actions separately.

The Judgment: The Great Slaughter in Bozrah

With the council at Adam-ondi-Ahman, the sixth seal closes, although some things overlap and continue into the seventh seal. The king of Assyria is gone. There are many of his followers still around, however, and they try for a short time to continue the kingdom of the beast. It comes to nothing because the terrible events of the last 42 months begin.

We have quoted many scriptures from Isaiah and there are many more we could have cited. He does not talk much about the last 42 months except at the beginning when the gathering takes place. But as far as the tremendous destruction that takes place in this period, we have to look elsewhere. John in his graphic Revelation, describes the calamities and woes in great detail. That is mainly where we get the knowledge of these events.

The Lord has sent these plagues and destruction upon the earth for two reasons: to destroy the wicked and to encourage people to repent. Because of this, the judgments become more severe and terrible as time passes until the remainder of mankind is destroyed completely except for those living in Old Jerusalem and in Zion. John begins the account:

> *And when he had opened the seventh seal, there was silence in heaven about the space of half an hour....The first angel sounded and there followed hail and fire mingled with blood and they were cast upon the earth: and the third part of trees was burn up, and all green grass was burnt up.* (Rev 8:1, 7)

At the beginning of the seventh seal, the next millennium, he says there is silence in heaven for a short time. We mentioned earlier that there was a period of peace which Isaiah mentions, when the antichrist or king of Assyria is destroyed. People begin to return to their native lands. But following this very short respite, the first of the seven angels sounds his trumpet and the first plague begins. This plague is a burning hail which destroys a third of the trees and all the green grass.

The question that arises here is whether or not John is speaking metaphorically. Trees and grass are metaphors for people throughout Isaiah and if we were reading that book, we would know that they are people. But John is not given to such metaphor in his descriptions. He is seeing a vision and describing what he sees. Later, he talks about men being killed and I doubt he would use a metaphor in one place and be literal in the same situation later.

In addition, we read in chapter 7 about this:

> *And I saw another angel ascending from the east, having the seal of the living God: and he cried with a loud voice to the four angels, to whom it was given to hurt the earth and the sea, Saying, Hurt not the earth, neither the sea, nor the trees, till we have sealed the servants of our God in their foreheads.* (Rev 7:2-3)

These angels are the first four angels who blow their trumpets and we know that this takes place after the sealing of the 144,000. These verses also make it clear that the hurting of the earth, which is not a metaphor, and the trees, etc. are literal. So what we are seeing is the beginning of the "hurting of the earth" by these messengers.

During this period, the entire face of the earth will be changed preparatory to its becoming a terrestrial earth during the Millennium. This is not to say that there is no symbolic coding, which we will see later.

This fire storm will have a devastating effect on the crops of the earth. It will apparently destroy all green plants which will result in great hunger. And this is just the first plague.

> *And the second angel sounded, and as it were a great mountain burning with fire was cast down into the sea: and the third part of the sea became blood. And the third part of the creatures which were in the sea, and had life, died; and the third part of the ships were destroyed.* (Rev 8:8-9)

The second angel likewise is one of the four who has power to hurt the earth and his plague comes in the form of a "mountain" falling out of the sky. John says mountain but it is obviously a huge meteorite or asteroid which comes down in one of the oceans. This kills a third of the marine life in the ocean and destroys a third of the ships.

It is interesting that today there is so much activity on the part of some groups of people to save the whales, dolphins and other marine life. Vast sums are spent on such activities while people starve in the cities. Eventually, all sea life will die, as we shall see. During the Millennium, there will be no oceans and therefore, no whales and dolphins. Just about all of these great and beautiful beasts have been born. The irony is that people who should know better, are worrying about the whales becoming extinct when God has already decreed their extinction.

Satan has deceived men and there are many faithful church members who are partisan to such propaganda. These people have put pressure on governments in past years to pass restrictive legislation ("unjust laws" Isaiah calls them) restricting the use of our natural resources, even though the Creator knew just how many we would need and we have not begun to use them up. Nor will we ever use them to depletion. A young elder I know gets furious when we talk of cutting down trees. He would join with those who take away our property rights and who follow Satan whose goal is to distort the truth and deceive men.

Our little children are being propagandized in school by LDS teachers in many cases. It is illegal to take a Bible into the schools which tells the truth about what will happen, but this Satanic and deceptive doctrine is made official and our little children come home with heads full of environmentalist nonsense.

There is more to come, however:

> *And the third angel sounded, and there fell a great star from heaven, burning as it were a lamp, and it fell upon the third part of the rivers, and upon the fountains of waters; And the name of the star is called Wormwood: and the third part of the waters became wormwood; and many men died of the waters, because they were made bitter.* (Rev 8:10-11)

Another giant fiery meteor or asteroid falls but this time on land and poisons the fresh water streams on a third of the land. This results in the death of many people. These things happen in quick succession. A third of the fish are destroyed, the crops are destroyed and now a third of the fresh water is poisoned. This will result in massive starvation. But remember that an average of 3.1 million people per day will have to die to depopulate the earth in 42 months in addition to the increase due to the birth rate.

With these great catastrophes having come upon men, they will no doubt be fighting for the dwindling food supplies. Mobs will ravage the land and add to the killing. People will eat their own offspring.

> *And the fourth angel sounded, and the third part of the sun was smitten, and the third part of the moon, and the third part of the stars; so as the third part of them was darkened, and the day shone not for a third part of it, and the night likewise.* (Rev 8:12)

The earth is cast out of its orbit and begins its trek across space to the place near Kolob where it was created. As this happens, the earth will "reel to and fro as a drunken man" (D&C 88:87). But at this time it is still near the sun and will probably slingshot around it. Isaiah gives some light on what is happening:

> *The day of the Lord shall come as a cruel outburst of anger and wrath to make the earth a desolation, that sinners may be annihilated from it. The stars and constellations of the heavens will not shine. When the sun rises, it shall be obscured; nor will the moon give its light. I have decreed calamity for the world, punishment for the wicked; I will put an end to the arrogance of insolent men and humble the pride of tyrants. I will make mankind scarcer than fine gold, men more rare than gold of Ophir. I will cause disturbance in the heavens when the earth is jolted out of place by the anger of the Lord of Hosts in the day of his blazing wrath. Then like a deer that is chased, or a flock of sheep that no one rounds up, each will return to his own people and everyone flee to his homeland. Whoever is found shall be thrust through; all who are caught shall fall by the sword. Their infants shall be dashed in pieces before their eyes, their homes plundered, their wives ravished.* (Isaiah 13:9-16)

This is what John is seeing. The Lord states his purpose is to annihilate all the sinners from the earth. This has never happened before except at the time of the flood in Noah's day long before this prophecy, so this scene described by Isaiah is still future. There will be great changes in the heavens. The Lord has said there will be a new heaven and a new earth and the changes John and Isaiah saw are going to cause that to happen. Included is the jolting out of place of the earth, or leaving its orbit which is necessary because it is traveling to be where it will probably remain for eternity.

Isaiah mentions that everyone will flee to his native land which will be a dangerous undertaking. There will be mobs and even the ordinary people will be dangerous. Everyone will be killing each other. This will be the worst time to have ever lived on the earth for most of humanity.

As we return to John's account, another angel announces more woe to come; three of them, to be exact:

And I beheld, and heard an angel flying through the midst of heaven, saying with a loud voice, Woe, woe, woe, to the inhabiters of the earth by reason of the other voices of the trumpet of the three angels, which are yet to sound! (Rev 8:13)

When the Lord says "woe" it is usually bad because he tends to understate things. The final three angels are about to sound the three final woes.

And the fifth angel sounded, and I saw a star fall from heaven unto the earth: and to him was given the key to the bottomless pit. And he opened the bottomless pit; and there arose a smoke out of the pit, as the smoke of a great furnace; and the sun and air were darkened by reason of the smoke of the pit. And there came out of the smoke locusts upon the earth: and unto them was given power, as the scorpions of the earth have power. And it was commanded them that they should not hurt the grass of the earth, neither any green thing, neither any tree; but only those men which have not the seal of God in their foreheads. And to them it was given that they should not kill them, but that they should be tormented five months: and their torment was as the torment of a scorpion, when he striketh a man. And in those days shall men seek death, and shall not find it; and shall desire to die, and death shall flee from them. And the shapes of the locusts were like unto battle; and on their heads were as it were crowns like gold, and their faces were as the faces of men. And they had hair as the hair of women, and their teeth were as the teeth of lions. And they had breastplates of iron; and the sound of their wings was as the sound of chariots of many horses running to battle. And they had tails like unto scorpions and there were stings in their tails and their power was to hurt men five months. And they had a king over them, which is the angel of the bottomless pit, whose name in the Hebrew tongue is Abaddon, but in the Greek tongue hath his name Apollyon. (Rev 9:1-11)

A very strange army now comes to vex men. This is a wondrous and mysterious prophecy which most non-Mormon scholars believe is just a fantasy and is something that will never happen. They believe that the plagues and woes in the Book of Revelation are simply figurative and meant to scare men into becoming more righteous.

LDS writers and scholars, while affirming they believe the book, have come up with preposterous explanations for this phenomenal woe. Of the current or past crop of last- days books, not one has been able to accurately explain this woe or the one to follow. The problem with trying to interpret this and other visions is that we tend to neglect some identifying facts and jump to the main graphic then try to figure out what it means in terms of our own experience. The only trouble with this is that no one has seen anything like this before.

When the fifth angel sounds, a star falls from heaven. This is an important identifier and image with which we are all familiar. Star is a metaphor for angel or children of our preexistent family. The star who fell was Lucifer, a star of the morning or one of the first born. Notice that he is not flying down, or descending but falling. With these rhetorical links we know he is Lucifer.

His fall was also in the preexistence. But at the time of the vision, the last days or the judgment period, he is given the key to the bottomless pit. This is the power to open this real or symbolic place. The bottomless pit is referred to by the Lord as the place where the unembodied followers of Lucifer live and where the mortal sons of perdition will eventually live with their brethren. They are not there now, however.

We know that these spirit followers are loose and free to roam the earth tempting mankind, but Lucifer has the key to release them from the bounds or scope of action in their condition. They are now given more power.

John sees smoke come out of the pit. This is woe in the form of the spirits who are there. John describes them as billowing out as smoke from a great furnace. They are concentrated in vast numbers. What are the numbers? We know that the number of unembodied spirits was a third of our God family. So half the number of all the people who will come to the earth to receive bodies is the number of Lucifer's followers. It was estimated that there have been only 50-to-60 billion people on the earth since the beginning starting with Adam and Eve. If there have been 50 billion plus the millions to be born during the Millennium, there are at least 25 billion and perhaps as many as 40 billion. They outnumber us at present at least five to one. At this time, however, much of mankind has died and we can assume that with the tribulation and the poisoning of the waters, death of the crops and the resulting famine, not nearly five billion remain.

These are Lucifer's followers who now have been given power for five months to physically torment mankind to the extent that people will be so sick and in such pain, they will desire to die but will not be able to do so. They will have power over all people except those who have the seal of God in their foreheads. These are the 144,000 who are abroad in the world to rescue any who repent and wish to join the Lord's people. They are translated at this time and impervious to any harm.

Another clue that they are Lucifer's spirits is found in Chapter 7. The use of the term "locust" is one the Lord used to describe the soldiers of the king of Assyria as he swarmed over the nations like caterpillars and locusts devouring everything as they went (Isaiah 33:3-4). The locust image is one describing the swarming of these devils but they are not nor do they look like locusts.

Spirits have the ability to appear in different forms. These spirits take the shapes of war horses. John says they have the faces of men, which identifies them as human creatures. They wear their hair long and have crowns like gold on their heads, and here is another clue.

The spirits pretend they are kings after the order of God but they are impostors and so the crowns they wear are also phony; not really gold but "like gold." They are wearing armor and have wings which make much noise. They have also designed tails with which they sting men. To be sure they are awesome looking creatures and to be feared. This is not a conventional army as most commentators have tried to describe. This is a real battle with the followers of Lucifer who are loosed for five months and then confined again.

> *And the sixth angel sounded, and I heard a voice from the four horns of the golden altar which is before God, saying to the sixth angel which had the trumpet, Loose the four angels which are bound in the bottomless pit. And the four angels were loosed, which were prepared for an hour, and a day, and a month, and a year, for to slay the third part of men. And the number of the army of the horsemen were two hundred thousand thousand: and I heard the number of them. And thus I saw the horses in the vision, and them that sat on them, having breastplates of fire, and of jacinth, and brimstone: and the heads of the horses were as the heads of lions; and out of their mouths issued fire and smoke and brimstone. By these three was the third part of men killed, by the fire, and by the smoke, and by the brimstone, which issued out of their mouths. For their power is in their mouth, and in their tails: for their tails were like unto serpents, and had heads, and with them they do hurt. And the rest of the men which were not killed by these plagues yet repented not of the works of their hands, that they should not worship devils, and idols of gold, and silver, and brass, and stone, and of wood: which neither can see, nor hear, nor walk: Neither repented they of their murders, nor of their sorceries, nor of their fornication, nor of their thefts.* (Rev 9:13-21)

Those who sought death and could not find it during the first woe, will now find it easily. There are obviously four powerful angels or devils, who are bound in the bottomless pit and are now loosed. These four powerful beings have an army which comes from the pit and so are of the same unembodied spirits as the first group. John tells us how many there are; 200 million. This is an elite group and very powerful.

John describes them as men mounted on horses who spewed fire and brimstone. They have power to slay by the mouth and by their tails which were like serpents. This army is turned loose for 13 months and eight days. Think of the joy they must feel to finally be able to slaughter mankind to their hearts' content. During their rampage, they will kill a third of mankind.

If there are three billion people still living, there will be a billion destroyed by these creatures. This is slaughter on such a grand scale that it defies comprehension. To destroy a billion people in 13 months will require the slaughter of about 2.5 million per day. Of course there is no way to know how many are still alive at this time; there could be fewer than three billion.

After the two woes, the people still refuse to repent. They are beyond repentance, however, and continue with their crimes for which they are being destroyed.

One of the major problems with any of the prophetic books lies in the chronology. The prophecies are often given without respect to time. A series of events can be given but entirely out of order. Because of this fact, we have to look for other guidelines and time checks. If we are diligent in our study, we eventually see the relationships and put them in their proper order. In most cases, we have to be familiar with other prophetic books where similar events have been described. Then we have to look for what I call time checks. These are places where the Lord through the particular prophet gives a time indication such as the beast having power for 42 months. Another is the fact that the beast is destroyed when the Ancient of days stands. By this we know that he will be destroyed when the council convenes. And so it is with Revelation.

As anyone can tell, Revelation is not written chronologically. It is a large chiasmus which has its center in chapters 12 and 13. A chiasmus, in the Hebrew mode which is different from chiasmus in modern writing, uses sets of parallel lines whose pairs are arranged in a vertical palindromic form so that it reads the same from top to bottom and from bottom to top with the climax in the center. A book can also be a chiasmus which Revelation is. John did not divide his book into chapters, however, but the relationship can be seen in the chapters as they are divided in our current version.

Revelation begins and ends with chapters that provide consolation for the faithful. There are chapters which detail John's mission in the last days which are placed both before and after chapters 12 and 13. The plagues and woes are divided with half coming before and half coming after. We now have ample time checks to distinguish and as we become accustomed to the this manner of Hebrew, or rather, the Lord's manner of giving revelation, it opens to our understanding and is as clear as any literal writing we have.

We mentioned the angel ascending from the east who is John. Later in the book we see another of his important missions which has been discussed before but this part is new:

> *And I looked, and behold a white cloud, and upon the cloud one sat like unto the Son of man, having on his head a golden crown, and in his hand a sharp sickle. And another angel came out of the temple, crying with a loud voice to him that sat on the cloud, Thrust in thy sickle, and reap: for the time is come for thee to reap; for the harvest of the earth is ripe. And he that sat on the cloud thrust in his sickle on the earth; and the earth was reaped. And another angel came out of the temple which is in heaven, he also having a sharp sickle. And another angel came out from the altar, which had power over fire; and cried with a loud cry to him that had the sharp sickle, saying, Thrust in thy sharp sickle, and gather the clusters of the vine of the earth; for her grapes are fully ripe. And the angel thrust in his sickle into the earth, and gathered the vine of the earth, and cast it into the great winepress of the wrath of God. And the winepress was trodden without the city, and blood came out of the winepress, even unto the horse bridles, by the space of a thousand and six hundred furlongs.* (Rev 14:14-20)

John sees a vision, the first part of which we have seen before as recorded by Daniel and discussed in Chapter 3:

> *I saw in the night visions, and, behold, one like the Son of Man came with the clouds of heaven, and came to the Ancient of Days, and they brought him near before them. And there was given him dominion and glory, and a kingdom, that all people, nations, and languages, should serve him:...* (Dan 7:13-14)

As we showed, this is the great Davidic king coming before Adam to receive his kingdom; the throne of David over Israel. Note the description: He came with the clouds and is like the Son of Man. John describes this same personage who is sitting on a cloud and has a gold crown on his head. In Daniel's vision, he is being given his kingdom but when John sees him (himself) he has his crown.

The cloud is a metaphor for judgment or tribulation. He, like the vision of the Savior, comes on a cloud because the mission represented by this metaphor is one of destruction.

He has a sickle in his hand which is a symbol of harvest. We also cited the verses from Isaiah where the Lord said:

> *I will make of you a sharp-toothed threshing sledge of new design, full of spikes: you shall thresh mountains to dust and make chaff of hills.* (Isaiah 41:15)

The Lord is speaking to the Davidic prophet/king and to his servants and he tells them they will be like a new design of a threshing sledge. In other words, they will be a destructive force, or rather the means they use to "thresh" will be radically different from any method yet seen. We have seen part of this already in the first four plagues by the four angels and the first two woes by the fifth and sixth angels which loosed the demons of the pit upon mankind to torment and slaughter them by the hundreds of millions.

The vision John sees is a sustaining of that same metaphor in which the Davidic king is seen with a sickle symbolically representing his reaping down of the world's population, both the good and the evil. The Lord's parable of the wheat and the tares is of this same time and is the same metaphor. The Lord commands his servants to allow the wheat and tares to grow together. At harvest time, they are all harvested together. The wheat is gathered into the barn and the tares are bundled and burned. Instead of bundles of wheat, this metaphor uses grapevines.

In every case, it is people who are being harvested. In the threshing sledge metaphor of Isaiah, the Lord says they will thresh mountains to dust and hills to chaff. As we have mentioned often, mountains and hills are nations and peoples. The returning to dust and chaff are chaos motifs used in the scriptures meaning they are uncreated or returned to the dust of the earth.

The earth is being reaped under the direction of the Davidic king and those who are with him, the 144,000. Their mission is to separate the remaining righteous, including the scattered of the House of Israel, from the vast masses of telestial order beings who are fated for annihilation.

The metaphor continues with the vines being cast into the winepress of the wrath of God. The details here are indicative of the magnitude of the slaughter. When the vines are pressed, blood comes out of the winepress as deep as horses bridles for a distance of 1600 furlongs. A furlong is an eighth of a mile so the distance is 200 miles. This is a lot of blood.

There is a story of a sacrifice performed by the Aztecs on a special feast day in Tenochtitlan in pre-Columbian times. The record states that by the end of the day, the priests were standing knee deep in blood and the ditches and gutters were filled. The amount given here is exaggerated. If you figure out the amount of blood in this vast a pool of about four feet deep and a radius of 200 miles, you will find it exceeds the amount of blood in the entire human population and in all the animals combined. This will include the rest of humanity.

There is an interesting note at the end of this passage. John says the winepress was "trodden without the city." This slaughter is not going on in the city which is New Jerusalem. The Lord himself will tread the winepress and there are ample scriptures affirming this fact and there is a mingling of metaphors here that is seldom discussed. In modern revelation the Lord mentions this metaphor several times of which the following is representative:

> *And the Lord shall be red in his apparel, and his garments like him that treadeth in the wine-vat. And his voice shall be heard: I have trodden the wine-press alone, and have brought judgment upon all people; and none were with me; And I have trampled them in my fury, and I did tread upon them in mine anger, and their blood have I sprinkled upon my garments, and stained all my raiment; for this was the day of vengeance which was in my heart.* (D&C 133:48, 50-51)

We are told that when he makes his descent in glory, he will be dressed in red as a symbol of that which is represented by the winepress metaphor. It is not a symbol only of the death of mankind. It is more complex than that. The central idea, that which makes Christianity alive and without which all devotion would be useless, is the atonement with its most moving symbol, the crucifixion. It is his own blood which was first shed in the winepress but by his own volition.

This is part of what he refers to as having trod the winepress alone. When he says that "none were with me" he is talking of this loneliest of events which only he could perform. By doing so he became the father and the son but he was already the creator in his persona as Jehovah. Likewise, only he had the right to bring the great judgment on the earth and slaughter those judged to be wicked and sinners. So the winepress treading began in Gethsemane and will end 2000 years later as the good and evil are separated in the winepress of the wrath of God. So this complex metaphor transcends and encompasses the entire scope of the creation, redemption and judgment of mankind.

> *Who is this coming from Edom in red-stained garments? Who is this from Bozrah, arrayed in majesty, pressing forward in the strength of his power? It is I, who am mighty to save, announcing righteousness! Why are you clothed in red, your garments like those who tread grapes in the winepress? Alone I have trodden out a vatful; of the nations no one was with me. I trod them down in my anger; in my wrath I trampled them. Their lifeblood spattered my garments, and I have stained my whole attire.* (Isaiah 63:1-3)

> *When my sword drinks its fill in the heavens, it shall come down on Edom in judgment, on the people I have sentenced to damnation. The Lord has a sword that shall engorge with blood and glut itself with fat—the blood of lambs and he-goats, the kidney fat of rams. For the Lord will hold a slaughter in Bozrah, an immense massacre in the land of Edom;* (Isaiah 34:5-6)

These verses are relevant to this event John is witnessing. In both these passages the Lord acknowledges his servant the Davidic king. In 63:1 he announces righteousness which is one of the names of the Davidic king. In the second he refers to him as his sword. We examined both these verses in talking about the Davidic king. He is the one who does the reaping. Here he is characterized as the sword.

The Lord states that he will come in red stained garments and restates the fact that he has trodden the winepress alone; the same statement he would make 2600 years later to Joseph Smith as we quoted from D&C 133.

The various beasts he mentions; lambs, he-goats, rams and later bisons, bulls and steers, represent classes of people from the humble, lowest classes to the highest of the people. All will taste the sword and participate in the great slaughter. Only two verses are quoted here but the entire Isaiah 34 is about this slaughter.

After this interlude, John sees another segment of the last days drama:

> *And I saw another sign in heaven, great and marvelous, seven angels having the seven last plagues; for in them is filled up the wrath of God. And one of the four beasts gave unto the seven angels seven golden vials full of the wrath of God, who liveth for ever and ever.* (Rev 15:1, 7)

John sees the seven angels who have the last seven plagues. This is important because we have already seen four terrible plagues poured out on the world in the form of natural disasters. In addition, we saw the two woes in which the demons from the pit were turned loose on mankind and a third of them were slain in the second woe.

Many commentators lump them together saying that the first seven and last seven are the same. This is not correct and a cursory reading will show that. They are similar in some respects but very different in others. These are new plagues that come, however, the third woe has not come and this woe comes at the end and is contemporary with the seventh angel who has the seventh vial.

> *And I heard a great voice out of the temple saying to the seven angels, Go your ways, and pour out the vials of the wrath of God upon the earth. And the first went, and poured out his vial upon the earth; and there fell a noisome and grievous sore upon the men which had the mark of the beast, and upon them which worshipped his image.* (Rev 16:1-2)

The Lord commissions the angels to pour out the plagues. These plagues are different from the first. In the first series, the first trumpet brought bloody hail which destroyed trees and all the green grass. This plague causes a bad sore on those who have the mark of the beast.

There has been very much speculation about the mark and this sore. People have theorized that the mark is anything from a tattoo to an implanted microchip. The fact that it causes a single sore rather than a rash or other illness, indicates that the two, the mark and the sore, are somehow related. This makes sense if the mark is some kind of embedded chip.

> *And the second angel poured out his vial upon the sea; and it became as the blood of a dead man: and every living soul died in the sea.* (Rev 16:3)

With the second plague we get something of a time check. When the second, third and fourth angels sounded their trumpets and their plagues struck the earth, great natural catastrophes occurred but only a third of the waters were damaged. In this plague, the waters of the sea become blood and all sea life dies.

There are many who say that the Lord could not destroy all the whales, dolphins and other marine life but the earth is being prepared for its terrestrial state and there will be no sea. This will be the condition during the Millennium. All the sea mammals who are destined to be born, have now come. There are no more to be born and so we need not be concerned with these matters. In spite of these revealed facts, there are many saints who are very much into the environmental movement. They either do not believe these prophecies or they are ignorant of them altogether. When I have suggested to people that the Creator knew exactly how many people would inhabit this planet and how many years it would endure, and that we do not need to worry about it, many have thought I was out of it and some have even gotten angry.

The environmental movement is largely Satan inspired to divert us from thinking about the last days and the signs. The Lord said that the righteous and meek would be looking forward to the signs of his coming (Rev 3:3; D&C 35:15; 39:23-24; 45:39; 49:23; 61:38 and others). Instead of looking eagerly for these signs, most members of the church in Utah are looking forth to the coming of the Olympics of 2002.

And the third angel poured out his vial upon the rivers and fountains of waters; and they became blood. And I heard the angel of the waters say, Thou art righteous, O Lord, which art, and wast, and shalt be, because thou hast judged thus. For they have shed the blood of saints and prophets, and thou hast given them blood to drink; for they are worthy. (Rev 16:4-6)

The third angel's plague is also very bad because it turns the fresh water to blood. This will destroy all fresh water life, although that is not mentioned here. This will leave the inhabitants of the earth in a bad way. Millions continue dying every day. Another angel affirms that the Lord's judgment is true in spite of this great slaughter.

> *And the fourth angel poured out his vial upon the sun; and power was given unto him to scorch men with fire. And men were scorched with great heat, and blasphemed the name of God, which hath power over these plagues: and they repented not to give him glory.* (Rev 16:8-9)

In the first series of plagues the sun was darkened but now is scorching hot. This may be due to the fact that the earth is now out of orbit and may be passing close to the sun as it slingshots around in a common space maneuver with which we are familiar in our space flights. At any rate, men will burn in the searing heat, but, as it says here, men will still not repent.

Men are being encouraged to repent by the plagues but also by the 144,000 who are still in the world trying to collect the last repentant stragglers. John says that men will not repent in spite of all this.

> *And the fifth angel poured out his vial upon the seat of the beast; and his kingdom was full of darkness; and they gnawed their tongues for pain, And blasphemed the God of heaven because of their pains and their sores, and repented not of their deeds.* (Rev 16:10-11)

The beast was destroyed about three years ago but the remainder of his kingdom still exists and the people are still there. It says that his kingdom is full of darkness. They are keeping alive the antichrist legacy and worship. The darkness here is spiritual darkness. These people will not repent after this plague. This is the only one of the plagues that is localized to a geographical area and it only affects those who are trying to perpetuate the kingdom of the beast, although it has little power.

> *And the sixth angel poured out his vial upon the great river Euphrates; and the water thereof was dried up, that the way of the kings of the east might be prepared.* (Rev 16:12)

We are now very near the time of Armageddon and preparations are made for the gathering of the remaining people at that place. This is the setup for the final destruction of all mankind who remain except for those who are in Zion and a small remnant in Jerusalem. This is metaphorical, of course. It would not be necessary to dry up a river so that people from the east could come. After all they have been traversing the globe for centuries and during the last seven years as well. River is a metaphor for an army. But in these times, a great river could be a barrier to moving people who now have few vehicles and fuel.

The river Euphrates begins in northern Turkey and flows down through Syria then bisects Iraq finally emptying into the north end of the Persian Gulf. Its length is nearly 2000 miles including the length after it joins with the Tigris which parallels the Euphrates beginning in Turkey, running the full length of Iraq, joining the Euphrates and ending together in the Persian Gulf. This river system provides a natural barrier between Israel and the rest of Asia. Due to the scorching heat, these rivers will literally be dried up.

The metaphor of the river Euphrates, however, represents the army of the Jews who call themselves Israel today. Their power will be broken so that they can no longer keep themselves from being overrun by the mobs and invading armies which will soon come. In addition, they have been protected by the power of the two witnesses who are present in Jerusalem during this 42-month period. We will discuss them later in this chapter. Somehow, their power will be broken or dried up by this sixth plague, which again is localized to the Jews.

> *At that time shall Michael stand up, the great prince which standeth for the children of thy people: and there shall be a time of trouble, such as never was since there was a nation even to that same time: and at that time thy people shall be delivered, everyone that shall be found written in the book....Then I Daniel looked, and, behold, there stood other two, the one on this side of the bank of the river, and the other on that side of the bank of the river. And one said to the man clothed in linen, which was upon the waters of the river, How long shall it be to the end of these wonders? And I heard the man clothed in linen, which was upon the waters of the river, when he held up his right hand and his left hand unto heaven, and sware by*

him that liveth for ever that is shall be for a time, times, and an half; and when he shall have accomplished to scatter the power of the holy people, all these things shall be finished. (Dan 12:1-3, 5-7)

So beginning with the great council, there is a time following which will see such trouble that nothing has ever been like it. The redemption of the people will come at the end of it. The angels or men speaking in Daniel's vision are discussing the events and the one asks how long this period of trouble will last. The other says a time, times and a half which is defined in Revelation and Daniel as 3-1/2 years. So here we get a time check and it shows that this period is 42 months as shown on the last days chart.

The relevant point to the sixth plague, however, is the fact that the power of the Jews, here called the holy people, is broken at the end of this period just before the end. But this is not the end of the sixth vial or plague:

And I saw three unclean spirits like frogs come out of the mouth of the dragon, and out of the mouth of the beast, and out of the mouth of the false prophet. For they are the spirits of devils, working miracles which go forth unto the kings of the earth and of the whole world, to gather them to the battle of that great day of God Almighty....And he gathered them together into a place called in the Hebrew tongue Armageddon. (Rev 16:13-16)

John sees the three evil spirits who possessed the dragon, the antichrist and the second beast or the false prophet as he is called here. The first is Satan himself because we were told in Chapter 13 that it was Satan who is the dragon. The dragon is the symbol of Satan. The other two are powerful demons who possessed the antichrist and the second beast who was the pope and his false religion which he transformed into the worship of the antichrist and of Satan.

These three spirits now go to the remaining kings, apparently in the east since the way is now clear for the kings of the east, to gather them to do battle against the Jews. The kings of the east and others are stirred up to destroy the Jews. It is interesting that Satan has kept alive the idea that the Jews are responsible for all the troubles of the world. This mistake will be made for the last time.

There is no such thing as the "battle of Armageddon" as it is popularly called. We are told here that the kings marshal their armies at that place. The Jews are not there. They are gathered in Jerusalem and are few in number by this time.

> *And the seventh angel poured out his vial into the air; and there came a great voice out of the temple of heaven, from the throne, saying, it is done. And there were voices, and thunders, and lightnings; and there was a great earthquake, such as was not since men were upon the earth, so mighty an earthquake, and so great. And the great city was divided into three parts, and the cities of the nations fell:...And every island fled away, and the mountains were not found. And there fell upon men a great hail out of heaven, every stone about the weight of a talent: and men blasphemed God because of the plague of the hail; for the plague thereof was exceeding great.* (Rev 16:17-21)

Thus ends the third woe and the seventh plague. We know they are one and the same, or at least happening simultaneously because both angels say it is finished. The hail puts an end to the invading armies and there is no battle. This is the final destruction of the remainder of mankind in the earth. The only people left alive are those in Zion, which is a large number and a handful in Jerusalem. We get some additional insights into these final actions from other scriptures:

> *And in that day will I make Jerusalem a burdensome stone for all people: all that burden themselves with it shall be cut in pieces, though all the people of the earth be gathered together against it. And it shall come to pass in that day, that I will seek to destroy all the nations that come against Jerusalem. And I will pour upon the house of David, and upon the inhabitants of Jerusalem, the spirit of grace and of supplications: and they shall look upon me whom they have pierced, and they shall mourn for him, as one mourneth for his only son, and shall be in bitterness for him, as one that is in bitterness for his firstborn.* (Zech 12:3, 8-10)

> *And it shall come to pass in that day, saith the Lord of hosts, that I will cut off the names of the idols out of the land, and they shall no more be remembered: and also I*

will cause the prophets and the unclean spirit to pass out of the land. And it shall come to pass, that when any shall yet prophesy, then his father and his mother that begat him shall say unto him, Thou shalt not live; for thou speakest lies in the name of the LORD: and his father and his mother that begat him shall thrust him through when he prophesieth. And it shall come to pass in that day, that the prophets shall be ashamed every one of his vision, when he hath prophesied; neither shall they wear a rough garment to deceive: But he shall say, I am no prophet, I am an husbandman; for man taught me to keep cattle from my youth. And one shall say unto him, What are these wounds in thine hands? Then he shall answer, Those with which I was wounded in the house of my friends. (Zech 13:2-6)

For I will gather all nations against Jerusalem to battle; and the city shall be taken, and the houses rifled, and the women ravished; and half of the city shall go forth into captivity, and the residue of the people shall not be cut off from the city. Then shall the Lord go forth, and fight against those nations, as when he fought in the day of battle. And his feet shall stand in that day upon the mount of Olives, which is before Jerusalem on the east, and the mount of Olives shall cleave in the midst thereof toward the east and toward the west, and there shall be a very great valley; and half of the mountain shall remove toward the north, and half of it toward the south. And ye shall flee to the valley of the mountains;...And this shall be the plague wherewith the Lord will smite all the people that have fought against Jerusalem; Their flesh shall consume away while they stand upon their feet, and their eyes shall consume away in their holes, and their tongue shall consume away in their mouth. (Zech 14:1-5, 12)

This is a very long quote but all of chapters 12-14 of Zechariah deal with this period and the last battle. Read them! He states that all nations will be gathered against Jerusalem in the last day, but he promises to destroy all who come against them. There are some interesting things that take place at this time that are not mentioned elsewhere.

We know that it is the end because the Lord appears to the

people and they ask what the wounds are in his hands. This is also quoted in modern revelation quoted below.

When the Lord appears, the people mourn because for 2000 years they have suffered persecution and death from having rejected their king and messiah. They will then begin to put the rabbis to the sword. Here they are called prophets but it refers to the religious leaders among the people. The people will be so angry to find out that they have been deceived for two millennia that even fathers and mothers will kill their sons if they start talking or teaching Judaism.

The gathering of all nations against Jerusalem which takes the city is the invasion by the archtyrant nearly seven years before when half are taken into captivity. But now the Lord is going to fight their battle.

There is a giant earthquake and the mount of Olives splits and forms a great valley. Half the city is destroyed and the survivors flee into the valley. In 13:8 (not quoted) the Lord says that two thirds of the people will be killed. There will not be many left.

> *And then shall the Jews look upon me and say: What are these wounds in thine hands and in thy feet? Then shall they know that I am the Lord; for I will say unto them: These wounds are the wounds with which I was wounded in the house of my friends....And then shall they weep because of their iniquities; then shall they lament because they persecuted their king.* (D&C 45:51-53)

This is the end of the judgment period. All of mankind who remain alive upon the earth are the people in Zion or New Jerusalem and the handful of Jews in Old Jerusalem. This is the final act before the coming of the Savior in glory dressed in red garments. The coming of the Savior will be in 45 days which we will discuss at the end.

The Gathering of Israel

One of the motivating ideas of the restoration in 1830 was the gathering of scattered Israel to the lands of their inheritance. The Lord stated that he had appointed the place for the gathering of his people at this time and the place has become a reverential object of hope and desire in the minds of the faithful. We speak of Jackson County as if it were Temple Square. We bought it; we own it; we will possess it some day.

Some foreign saints have become perplexed in the past few decades because the gathering which they thought should be taking place, is not happening. They read the revelations given to the church at this time and wonder.

> *Mine indignation is soon to be poured out without measure upon all nations; and this will I do when the cup of their iniquity is full. And in that day all who are found upon the watch-tower, or in other words, all mine Israel, shall be saved. And they that have been scattered shall be gathered. Zion shall not be moved out of her place, notwithstanding her children are scattered. They that remain, and are pure in heart, shall return, and come to their inheritances, they and their children, with songs of everlasting joy, to build up the waste places of Zion...And, behold, there is none other place appointed than that which I have appointed; neither shall there be any other place appointed than that which I have appointed, for the work of the gathering of my saints—...* (D&C 101:11-13, 17-18, 20)

The Lord says more about this in the famous Section 45:

> *And the remnant shall be gathered unto this place;...and the saints shall come forth from the four quarters of the earth. Then shall the arm of the Lord fall upon the nations....And it shall be called the New Jerusalem, a land of peace, a city of refuge, a place of safety for the saints of the Most High God; And the glory of the Lord shall be there, and the terror of the Lord also shall be there, insomuch that the wicked will not come unto it, and it shall be called Zion. And it shall come to pass among the wicked, that every man that will not take his sword against his neighbor must needs flee unto Zion for safety. And there shall be gathered unto it out of every nation under heaven; and it shall be the only people that shall not be at war one with another....And it shall come to pass that the righteous shall be gathered out from among all nations, and shall come to Zion, singing with songs of everlasting joy.* (D&C 45:43, 46-47, 66-69, 71)

Saints in foreign countries have read these verses and wondered when the time will be. These verses give us a hint. The gathering will occur just before the "arm of the Lord" falls upon the nations. This we know to be the Davidic king, the angel John saw with the sickle in his hand. The gathering is part of the harvest but it comes at the beginning so the righteous are spared the destructions and plagues in the nations. While all people are fighting each other, the righteous of Israel and other righteous people will be gathered to Zion.

> *Go ye out from Babylon. Be ye clean that bear the vessels of the Lord....Yea, verily I say unto you again, the time has come when the voice of the Lord is unto you: Go ye out of Babylon; gather ye out from among the nations, from the four winds, from one end of heaven to the other....Let them, therefore, who are among the Gentiles flee unto Zion. And let them who be of Judah flee unto Jerusalem, unto the mountains of the Lord's house. Go ye out from among the nations, even from Babylon, from the midst of wickedness, which is spiritual Babylon. But verily, thus saith the Lord, let not your flight be in haste, but let all things be prepared before you; and he that goeth, let him not look back lest sudden destruction shall come upon him.* (D&C 133:5, 7, 12-15)

The Lord here commands the scattered of Israel to gather themselves out. This will be in the future and we will see from Isaiah some specific details of the gathering. At present, there are many saints who would gather here to the United States and specifically to Utah if they were permitted.

The immigration laws have been changed in the past several decades to prevent immigration from the western nations and to encourage immigration from third world countries. This is part of the globalist move to mix the peoples, especially those of the industrialized nations. This is why we have seen huge ghettos spring up in our major cities. There are large populations of oriental, African and southeastern European peoples.

There are saints I have spoken with in Europe and England, who are of Ephraim and who have applied for immigration to the United States. Most have waited for years without success.

Many of the others who have come here are refugees from wars and upheaval in their countries. The United States is the great grantor of asylum to these people. Following the Vietnam war, the US government allowed hundreds of thousands of refugees from there into this country. They were mostly people who worked for the United States forces, were friendly to us and the South Vietnamese cause and were government workers or families thereof. The US government had an obligation to these people it had abandoned and their coming is just. Some so-called refugees from other areas have doubtful justification. Many are simply fleeing from economic or other internal difficulties. Such a case was the Haitian boat people. They were returned to Haiti on the grounds that they were only economic refugees.

The reason I mention all this is that the Lord in the verses just quoted, said "...let them, therefore, who are among the Gentiles flee unto Zion. And let them that be of Judah flee unto Jerusalem, unto the mountains of the Lord's house." (D&C 133:12-13). This may be the Lord's action and a method of bringing certain people to the "mountains of the Lord's house." We know that mountain means nation. There are two nations where the Lord's house, the house of Israel, are being gathered. So his decree may be in process of being carried out at this time.

The righteous of Israel who are in Vietnam, could very well all be among the refugees who come to this land even though they have not yet been identified as Israel and have not accepted the gospel. The work among the Vietnamese people is proceeding and many stakes of the church, mine included, have thriving Vietnamese branches and wards. The same is true with some other ethnic groups.

My old mission president's favorite hymn, which we sang at every mission conference because of its great message, was "God Moves In A Mysterious Way." His philosophy was that the Lord can bring to pass marvelous things in a way we cannot suspect because of our finite wisdom. I think the Lord is setting up conditions which will make the gathering easier for some people, but this is just my opinion. The events associated with the gathering are spelled out in scripture, however.

There are two parts to the gathering and sometimes they are confused by people who know about them. The first part of the gathering is the exodus which was discussed in detail in Chapter Two. The last days exodus takes place at the beginning of the tribulation period and consists only of a small group of Ephraim and a few people from other tribes who are with Ephraim. These are the small righteous remnant of the church who are not in apostasy and who are characterized by the wise virgins in the parable of that name. They are taken in one day/night into the wilderness where Zion is born in a day. The exodus lasts about three years ending in Zion by the end of the tribulation period. The adult males on the exodus will be sealed and become the 144,000 who, with the Davidic prophet/king will gather the rest of Israel and other righteous people to Zion and to Judah.

The gathering is an event which will take place beginning with the end of the tribulation when the Davidic king is crowned at Adam-ondi-Ahman and the 144,000 are sealed. The gathering will be done by the Davidic prophet and the 144,000 who will go into the world during the judgment period, described in the preceding section, preaching and bringing out the repentant and also the Ten Tribes. The specific gathering of the Ten Tribes was covered in Chapter Three.

In the following discussion, the general business and events of the gathering will be covered with extensive citations from Isaiah who talks about this event. The many citations from Isaiah are necessary because it is assumed that few readers of this work are familiar with the unsealed version.

> *In that day the sprig of Jesse, who stands for an ensign to the peoples, shall be sought by the nations, and his residence shall be glorious. In that day my Lord will again raise his hand to reclaim the remnant of his people—those who shall be left out of Assyria, Egypt, Pathros, Cush, Elam, Shinar, Hamath, and the islands of the sea. He will raise the ensign to the nations and assemble the exiled of Israel; he will gather the scattered of Judah from the four directions of the earth....And there shall be a pathway out of Assyria for the remnant of his people who shall be left, as there was for Israel when it came up from the land of Egypt.* (Isaiah 11:10-12, 16)

The Davidic king will be an ensign to the peoples. He will be recognized by all nations. We read previously that kings would bow when he passed by. His residence is New Jerusalem, the new city of David. He (the Lord) will raise his hand (the Davidic king) to gather the people. The Lord gives a list of metaphorical names of countries, most of which we cannot identify without some study. We know Egypt, Assyria and Cush but the others take some study and inspiration. The point is that he will bring the scattered people of Israel from wherever they are in the earth, including the most remote village in the most remote mountains. There will be wondrous signs that accompany the gathering. In this passage, he mentions a pathway out of Assyria, which is called a highway elsewhere.

We have not had time to do all the missionary work necessary to gather all of scattered Israel. We have only been allowed into some countries in the past five years. They will have to come out in a very short time which will require some miraculous assistance. This will come in the form of translated beings with great power, the 144,000 led by the one mighty and strong, the Davidic king.

> *Rejoice not, all you Philistines, now that the rod which struck you is broken. From among the descendants of that snake shall spring up a viper, and his offspring shall be a fiery flying serpent. The elect poor shall have pasture, and the needy recline in safety. But your descendants I will kill with famine, and your survivors shall be slain....What shall then be told the envoys of the nation? The Lord has founded Zion; let his longsuffering people find refuge there.* (Isaiah 14:29-30, 32)

We know from the previous chapter that the viper is the Davidic prophet/king and the fiery flying serpent, the offspring of the snake (Christ) are the 144,000. They will gather the people to the refuge which is Zion. This will occur after the tribulation, hence he calls them "his longsuffering people."

> *In that day the Lord will thresh out his harvest from the torrent of the River to the streams of Egypt. But you shall be gleaned one by one, O children of Israel. In that day a loud trumpet shall sound, and they who were lost in the land of Assyria and they who were outcasts in the land of Egypt shall come and bow down to the Lord in the holy mountain at Jerusalem.* (Isaiah 27:12-13)

The Lord, using the harvest metaphor, explains that the children of Israel will be gathered out one by one. The torrent of the

River is the great army and people of the king of Assyria, or Russia. The Lord will gather the people from all parts of the earth from the populations of the United States and Russia and everyone between. He especially mentions the ones lost in the land of Assyria, referring to the lost tribes and perhaps many of Ephraim.

The ones who were outcasts in Egypt are the members of the church today. The church was expelled from the United States and finally taken over by the government. This is similar to what happened to Israel in ancient Egypt. They were considered evil and a cancer on the body politic which needed to be excised. The governor of Illinois issued an extermination order against the Mormon vermin. It may be asked why the Lord refers to the members of the church as needing to be gathered.

We mentioned that the exodus will only involve five percent of the membership of the church. This left 95 percent still living in Utah and neighboring states, along with the many members of the church in other countries. The members in the United States are the ones specifically referred to here, however. They (we) are the ones who have been outcasts in our own land, which is Egypt.

The people of the church who do not go on the exodus will have to go through the captivity by the king of Assyria and suffer the tribulation for the 42 months of his conquest of the world. He also speaks to those who are in other lands.

> *Let not the foreigner who adheres to the Lord say, The Lord will surely exclude me from his people. And let not the eunuch say, I am but a barren tree. For thus says the Lord: As for the eunuchs who keep my Sabbaths and choose to do what I will—holding fast to my covenant—to them I will give a handclasp and a name within the walls of my house that is better than sons and daughters; I will endow them with an everlasting name that shall not be cut off. And the foreigners who adhere to the Lord to serve him, who love the name of the Lord, that they may be his servants—all who keep the Sabbath without profaning it, holding fast to my covenant—these I will bring to my holy mountain and gladden in my house of prayer. Their offerings and sacrifices shall be accepted on my altar, for my house shall be known as a house of prayer for all nations. Thus says my Lord the Lord who gathers*

up the outcasts of Israel: I will gather others to those already gathered. (Isaiah 56:3-8)

The door is open to foreigners or Gentiles as well as Israel. He uses the example of eunuchs who, though barren, if they receive the covenant will be able to enter the temple where the Lord will endow them with something that is better than sons and daughters. Even though they do not have children in this life, they will be anointed to become gods and have eternal increase.

The important point here is that they will be received and gathered to Zion along with other foreigners to join those already gathered, or Ephraim.

In a dramatic passage in which the prophet speaks for the people, the exiled ones, we get a feeling for their plight:

Then his people recalled the days of Moses of old: Where is he who brought them up out of the Sea with the shepherd of his flock? Where is he who put into him his holy Spirit, who made his glorious arm proceed at the right hand of Moses, who divided the waters before them, making an everlasting name for himself when he led them through the deep? Like the horse of the desert, they stumbled not; like cattle descending the slopes of ravines, it was the Spirit of the Lord that guided them. So thou didst lead they people, O Lord, acquiring illustrious renown. O look down from heaven from they holy and glorious celestial abode, and behold! Where now are thy zeal and thy might? The yearnings of thy bosom and thy compassion are withheld from us! Surely thou art our Father Though Abraham does not know us or Israel recognize us, thou, O Lord, art our Father; Our Redeemer from Eternity is thy name. Why, O Lord, hast thou made us stray from thy ways, hardening our hearts so that we do not fear thee? Relent, for the sake of thy servants, the tribes that are thine inheritance. But a little while had they people possessed the holy place when our enemies trod down the sanctuary. We have become as those whom thou has never ruled and who have not been known by thy name. (Isaiah 63:11-19)

In this fictional monologue, the Lord explains the plight of the scattered people of the tribes of Israel as though they were speaking. Eventually, they come to a remembrance of the early days when Israel was born in the day they left Egypt of old led by Moses and "his glorious arm" who was the preexistent Davidic prophet, John the apostle, known then as the Angel of his Presence.

The idea here is that God did all these things for the tribes of Israel in the beginning and they are begging him to now look down in compassion on the people who are the posterity of those original people. They are saying that Abraham does not know them or Israel recognize them. In other words, they are not known to modern Israel today. They are anonymous and lost as far as anyone is concerned.

They make a poignant appeal for the Lord to relent and rescue these tribes. They also ask why the Lord hardened their heart. He of course did not do this, but rather, they were mislead by their leaders and rabbis to break the covenant. They now appeal to the Lord through the terms of the Davidic covenant, which they have not kept, to save them. They finally lament that they had barely possessed the holy land when their enemies came and carried them into captivity and obscurity.

While it is not stated, the Lord is saying all this to indicate that the covenantal relationship will be reestablished through their new king, the Davidic prophet, and he will lead them back to the "holy place" once again under the terms of the modern Davidic covenant. In other places he responds to this plea:

> *The Lord has bared his holy arm in the eyes of all nations, that all ends of the earth may see our God's salvation. Break out all together into song, you ruined places of Jerusalem: the Lord has comforted his people; he has redeemed Jerusalem. Turn away, depart; touch nothing defiled as you leave Babylon. Come out of her and be pure, you who bear the Lord's vessels. But you shall not leave in haste or go in flight: the Lord will go before you, the God of Israel behind you. My servant, being astute, shall be highly exalted; he shall become exceedingly eminent: just as he appalled many—his appearance was marred beyond human likeness, his semblance unlike that of men—So shall he yet astound many nations, rulers shutting their mouths at him—what was not told them, they shall see; what they had not heard, they shall consider.* (Isaiah 52:9-15)

Part of this was commented upon in relation to the Davidic king to whom this refers. Following the great council, the Davidic king, fully empowered, will be seen and recognized by all nations, except possibly by the Jews who just finished rejecting him. The reason is because he is the herald of salvation, which is the name of the Savior. In other words, he is sent into the world to reveal and herald the Savior's coming. He is, after all, Elias.

The Lord calls upon the people to break out in song, which is worship, because the Lord has redeemed Jerusalem, which is Zion, the people of the Lord, or Israel. He counsels the people being gathered to come out of Babylon and not touch anything defiled. These people are they who bear the vessels of the Lord. Vessels are metaphors for children, so they are they who bear the Lord's children, his holy offspring. They are holy because they are special spirits reserved for this time when they will not be tempted but rather will grow up sinless.

The Lord promises he will go before the people and behind them as they gather. He further tells them not to leave in haste. The gathering will be an orderly event in spite of the fact that the judgments are commencing of which we read in the previous section.

We commented on these last verses in our coverage of the Davidic prophet. The Davidic prophet will be highly exalted. When he was taken and imprisoned, he was tortured and mutilated to the extent that he no long appeared to be human. But when he is exalted, all will be astounded and rulers of nations, what remain of them, will shut their mouths at him. They will not be able to speak to him. His wisdom or astuteness will baffle them. He will tell them what they have not seen nor heard. This is the gospel augmented by much new knowledge. The awe that is accorded him by the kings of the nations will be important in the gathering too.

We also covered the calling of the Davidic prophet in Isaiah 49:5-8 where the Lord told him it was his mission to raise up the tribes of Israel and restore them to their lands. Beginning with verse 9, the gathering is described as the Lord continues:

> *...to say to the captives, Come forth! and to those in darkness, Show yourselves! They shall feed along the way and find pasture on all barren heights; they shall not hunger or thirst, nor be smitten by oppressive heat or by the sun:*

> *he who has mercy on them will guide them; he will lead them by springs of water. All my mountain ranges I will appoint as roads; my highways shall be on high. See these, coming from afar, these, from the northwest, and these, from the land of Sinim. Shout for joy, O Heavens; celebrate, O earth! Burst into song, O mountains! The Lord is comforting his people, showing compassion for his afflicted. But Zion said, The Lord has forsaken me, my Lord has forgotten me. Can a woman forget her suckling infant, or feel no compassion for the child of her womb? Although these forget, I will not forget you. See, I have engraved you on my palms; have sealed you to be continually before me. Your sons shall hasten your ravagers away—those who ruined you shall depart from you. Lift up your eyes and look around you; with one accord they gather and come to you. As surely as I live, says the Lord, you shall adorn yourself with them all as with jewels, bind them on you as does a bride. For your ruins and ravaged places, and your land laid waste, shall now be too small for your inhabitants, despite the departure of your devourers. The children born during the time of your bereavement shall yet say in your ears, This place is too cramped for us; give us space in which to settle! And you will say to yourself, Who bore me these while I was bereaved and barren? I was exiled, banished; by whom were these reared? When I was left to myself, where were they? Thus says my Lord the Lord: I will lift up my hand to the nations, raise my ensign to the peoples; and they will bring your sons in their bosoms and carry your daughters on their shoulders. Kings shall be your foster fathers, queens your nursing mothers. They will bow down before you, their faces to the ground; they will lick the dust of your feet. Then shall you know that I am the Lord, and that they who hope in me are not disappointed.* (Isaiah 49:9-23)

The Davidic prophet will say to the captives, "Come forth!" He is in the world bringing those who have been in captivity to freedom. The double meaning is obvious. First the people of the world have been in captivity to the beast for 42 months. The

Davidic prophet literally frees them by killing the archtyrant and scattering his forces destroying many or most of them. Because of this victory, his fame will spread throughout the world. He will be greatly admired by all peoples.

He is also freeing the captives who are ignorant of the truth, or those who are in spiritual darkness, as we say. We quoted from Isaiah earlier when he said that the leaders of nations would hear things they had not heard. This is the gospel in its fulness with all truth restored, which is one of the missions of the Davidic prophet, and minus the myths that have crept in over the years.

The Lord continues and describes the journey back to Zion using a cattle metaphor. The image is one of grazing cattle who feed along the way as they travel including on barren heights. The Lord promises to feed the returnees and give them water along with protecting them from the sun. They will be traveling away from the centers of population and will be in the wilderness moving toward Zion under the direction of various members of the 144,000 who are now terrestrial beings of great power. They will provide for the people in miraculous ways.

In these verses the Lord is addressing Zion, the metaphorical wife, and she had been lamenting because the Lord, her husband, had forgotten her. He then tells her to look around because the exiles are coming from everywhere, from the northwest and even from the land of Sinim, which is China. They are metaphorically compared to jewels with which Zion will adorn herself as a bride. He says the land will now be too small for all Zion's inhabitants.

Zion wonders where all the children came from during her exile and bareness. During the time of the apostasy, there were no offspring of the Lord and his bride, the church. But now that she is restored and made glorious, she wonders at the great host of offspring that are now being gathered. "Being left alone" refers to the Jews especially, who think they are the only ones left of Zion, or God's only people. They will be amazed to see they are a small minority at this time. That is why she asks, "Who bore these while I was bereaved and barren?"

The gathering will be assisted by Gentiles as well. He says he will lift up his "hand" and raise his "ensign," both names of the Davidic prophet. The nations will respond by helping the people return home. Maybe they will want them to go when they find out they are of the tribes of Israel. This is likely. But these exiles are not only of Israel, but they have recognized the fact through the teaching and gathering of the Davidic prophet and the 144,000 and are now repentant and righteous people in contrast to the majority of the world's inhabitants. It is more likely that the Gentiles will initially feel a great sense of gratitude to the Davidic prophet who released them from the bonds of the archtyrant. In this setting, many will, no doubt, want to assist him as he requests.

There will be great manifestations of power by the Davidic prophet and the 144,000 servants, and the kings and queens of nations will bow down to them, licking the dust of their feet. This is either very great respect, which just does not seem possible, or great fear which is probably the case. The latter seems more reasonable because in a few months, these kings and queens will amass their followers at Jerusalem to annihilate the Jews. But, at least during the gathering, they will be helping the people to leave and return to either Jerusalem or to Zion.

In the days of the original king David, he was loved by the people for his exploits but hated by Saul and those in power, although they could not openly and publicly oppose him. The Lord says this will be a sign to the people and they will know that he is the Lord. Later in another verse in the same chapter, not quoted above, he says:

> *Can the warrior's spoil be taken from him, or the tyrant's captives escape free? Yet thus says the Lord: The warrior's spoil shall indeed be taken from him, and the tyrant's captives escape free: I myself will contend with your contenders, and I will deliver your children. I will feed your oppressors with their own flesh; they shall be drunk with their own blood as with wine. And all flesh shall know that I the Lord am your Savior, that your Redeemer is the Valiant One of Jacob.* (Isaiah 49:24-26)

The archtyrant will be so powerful that he will conquer the entire world and bring all people into captivity or domination. The question is, can he be defeated and his captives and spoil be taken from him? The Lord answers his own question and says it will be done and he will deliver her children, that is the children of Zion.

The people who took them captive will eat their own flesh

either literally or metaphorically by the sword. As we saw in the previous section, there will be widespread famine as the plagues begin to ravish the world. This may also be another motive for letting the people of Israel go. Since there is not enough food, they will probably be happy to see these groups of people depart. Those who enslaved them will soon be reduced to cannibalism to survive. All will recognize the Lord in all the nations. This is also brought about by the Davidic king and the 144,000.

> *For I will come to gather all nations and tongues, that they may approach and behold my glory. And I will set a mark upon them, sending those of them who survive to the nations that had not heard the news concerning me, nor seen my glory—to Tarshish, Pul, and Lud (the archers), to Tubal and Javan, and to the distant isles. And they shall declare my glory among the nations and shall bring back all your brethren from throughout the nations to Jerusalem my holy mountain, says the Lord, as offerings to the Lord—on horses, in chariots and wagons, and on mules and dromedaries—just as the Israelites brought offerings in pure vessels to the house of the Lord. Of them likewise I will accept men to be priests and Levites, says the Lord.* (Isaiah 66:18-21)

Those who survive are the people of the exodus. It is not a lottery, but rather, the band of survivors is taken and they become survivors by the fact that they were righteous and prepared. They are the wise virgins explained in Chapter Two. If they were the only survivors in the sense of the only ones left, how could they go into the world and gather the Lord's children who are also survivors? They are escapees rather than survivors in the sense we use the word today. They are sent to the so-called heathen nations or non-Christian countries who know nothing of the Lord. Even in the Christian countries, most are now worshippers of the beast, although he is dead.

Isaiah gives additional description of the returning exiles in many places. A few citations will be instructive:

> *Though my Lord give you the bread of adversity and the water of affliction, yet shall your Teacher remain hidden no longer, but your eyes shall see the Master. Your ears shall hear words from behind you saying, This is the way;*

walk in it! should you turn left or right. On all mountain heights and prominent hills shall appear streams of running water, on the day of the great slaughter, when the towers fail. The light of the moon shall be as the light of the sun, and the light of the sun increase sevenfold; as the light of seven days shall it be, in the day the Lord binds up the fracture of his people and heals their open wound. Behold the Lord Omnipotent coming from afar! His wrath is kindled,...But for you there shall be singing, as on the night when a festival commences, and rejoicing of heart, as when men march with flutes and drums and lyres; on their way to the mountain of the Lord, to the Rock of Israel. (Isaiah 30:20, 25-29)

The people of Israel, as with the rest of the world, suffered under the yoke of the king of Assyria but now the scene changes. He uses the mountain and water metaphors again to tell us that the people (streams of running water) will appear in all nations (mountains and hills). The people being gathered will be on the move.

At this time a great transformation is taking place. The earth is being changed from a telestial to a terrestrial world. We read about the scorching heat that comes but the Lord protects them from the heat as we read above. In addition, Zion will already be transformed because of the many terrestrial and celestial beings who are there, including the Lord. The Lord refers to this as "the day of the great slaughter."

The fracture of the people is the division between Ephraim and Judah which goes back more than 3000 years. This will be healed and they will become one people. The Jews, or the small group still in Jerusalem, will be converted when they see him at the end of the judgment period. There are many Jews who will have previously been converted as we discussed in earlier chapters. At the time of the appearance of the Savior, there will be few Jews remaining alive in Jerusalem.

It will be like Mardi Gras when they come to Zion singing as though it were a festival. This presents a great contrast to the weeping and gnawing of tongues which is beginning in the rest of the world.

See, my Lord the Lord comes with power; his arm presides for him. His reward is with him; his work precedes him. Like a shepherd he pastures his flock: the lambs he gathers up with his arm and carries in his bosom; the ewes that give milk he leads gently along. (Isaiah 40:10-11)

Everything is being accomplished now with great power. Arm, as we know, is a name for the Davidic prophet, who presides for the Lord with all the keys. Two other metaphors are used in the second sentence, reward and work. Reward is redemption. This the Lord brings with him. Those gathered out are not only saved from the judgment but are also given salvation. These people will be saved in a kingdom of glory, either the celestial or the terrestrial. They have now earned this.

Work, is his "marvelous work and a wonder" which is the judgment or vengeance on the world. The vengeance and destruction are going on, or preceding him but his reward is with him which he will give to those who are gathered to Zion. The reward is eternal life.

The shepherd image is used here to show the gentleness of the Davidic prophet as he brings the people to Zion. This reference is particularly of the exodus, but the people of the gathering will come in much the same way.

I will lay waste mountains and hills and make all their vegetation wither; I will turn rivers into dry land and evaporate lakes. Then will I lead the blind by a way they did not know, and guide them in paths unfamiliar; the darkness confronting them I will turn into light, and the uneven ground make level. These things I will not fail to perform. (Isaiah 42:15-16)

The mountains and hills, or nations and peoples, are laid waste by the king of Assyria and by the judgment that follows. The vegetation is the people who wither in this destruction, or in other words, they die. He uses the standard Isaiahic metaphors to describe the destruction. He uses the water metaphor again here. The rivers and lakes will be dried. These are also people. Rivers are generally armies and lakes are large populations.

As all this is happening, the blind, or those who were in darkness as we read above, are led out. These are the scattered of Israel, the Ten Tribes, the Jews and the Lamanites who make up most of scattered Israel. By contrast he will lead them in paths they have not known.

The Lord physically turns the darkness to light by his glory or canopy, but the Davidic king and the 144,000 will also teach them the truth which dispels that form of blindness or ignorance. This is done by the Davidic prophet, who is, as the Lord promised him, a light to the nations also.

Making the uneven ground level is a metaphor for the coming of the Lord as well as a literal occurrence of this period.

Notwithstanding the great oppression of the tyrant, the Lord promises to redeem his people in the end.

> *Let the ransomed of the Lord return! Let them come singing to Zion, their heads crowned with everlasting joy; let them obtain joy and gladness, and sorrow and sighing flee away. I myself am your Comforter. Who are you that you fear mortal man, the children of men who shall be turned to grass? Have you forgotten the Lord, your maker—who suspends the heavens, who sets the earth in place—that you go all day in constant dread of the oppressor's rage as he readies himself to wreak destruction? What is there to the wrath of the oppressor? Soon now shall he who is bowed down be set free; he shall not die as those destined for the Pit, neither shall he want for food.* (Isaiah 51:11-14)

These verses give consolation and comfort to the oppressed who are beneath the yoke of the tyrant, the antichrist. He berates the people for fearing the tyrant who will soon be turned to grass. Grass is a metaphor for people but the Lord will turn this grass to dust. He reminds us that he is the Almighty Creator and comforter and that instead of walking around all day in fear, we should remember him. He is the other comforter, the Holy Spirit of Promise. It is he who seals the blessings of the covenant by accepting us. It is he who crowns the heads with everlasting joy, which is the realization of the blessings promised in the holy place.

Verse 13 may need some explanation because it may be unclear who is about to wreak destruction. This is the Lord, the subject of the sentence. He asks why we go in fear when the Lord is about to wreak the awful destruction we have read as revealed by John in Revelation. It is he we should fear.

Finally, the Lord promises to free his captive people and they will live and have food. Remember that during the tribulation period there will be severe food shortages and no one can buy or sell without the mark of the beast.

Those who are finally freed will come to Zion in joy. This is a continual theme in Isaiah. At the beginning of the book the Lord gives the promise of great joy to those who survive.

> *In that day the plant of the Lord shall be beautiful and glorious, and the earth's fruit the pride and glory of the survivors of Israel. Then shall they who are left in Zion and they who remain in Jerusalem be called holy—all who were inscribed to be among the living at Jerusalem. This shall be when my Lord has washed away the excrement of the women of Zion and cleansed Jerusalem of its bloodshed, in the spirit of justice, by a burning wind. Over the whole site of Mount Zion, and over its solemn assembly, the Lord will form a cloud by day and a mist glowing with fire by night: above all that is glorious shall be a canopy. It shall be a shelter and shade from the heat of the day, a secret refuge from the downpour and from the rain.* (Isaiah 4:2-6)

The plant of the lord is the vine metaphor from the parable of the vineyard and the olive tree. Zion is the plant of the Lord and it will be made glorious. Those who survive, and certainly not all will survive, will be made glorious, that is, have their call and election made sure and ultimately be glorified.

One of the things that has made Isaiah extremely difficult to understand is his use of metaphor throughout the book. Metaphors were used extensively to seal the book so that evil men could not take precious parts out, since they, themselves, did not understand the book. One such metaphor is "Jerusalem." But, I hear you say, Jerusalem is a contemporary city today so how can it be a metaphor?

Jerusalem was the capital and center of the Lord's people for hundreds of years, especially after the captivity of Israel, the northern kingdom. Due to this fact, the Lord can address his people as Jerusalem. In the latter days, the center of the Lord's people where his keys and authority are found, is in Salt Lake City and other places where there are authorized officials. Jerusalem anciently meant Jerusalem and the land and cities around who received their authority from Jerusalem.

The keys and authority were taken from that place after the death of the apostles and disappearance of the church there. In the latter days, the keys and authority were restored and given to Ephraim. Since the prophecies of Isaiah pertain to the last days and to Israel, Jerusalem refers to the seat of authority in these times. To make a long explanation short, Jerusalem, in most cases in Isaiah refers to the church or gathered Ephraim today.

In these verses just cited, he says that Jerusalem, or the church, has to be cleansed of its filth and bloodshed. Most of these things were covered in Chapter 1 and I will not discuss them here. The first three chapters of Isaiah deal with the latter-day apostasy in detail.

Those of the church who remain alive will be the righteous ones who will then be called holy. This should dispel the notion that the church as a whole will be spared the tribulation. Not only will 95 percent of the church have to pass through the tribulation but few will remain. Isaiah gives us an idea of the relative numbers:

> *For the Lord will drive men away and great shall be the exodus from the centers of the land. And while yet a tenth of the people remain in it, or return, they shall be burned. But like the terebinth or the oak when it is felled whose stump remains alive, so shall the holy offspring be what is left standing.* (Isaiah 6:12-13)

During the invasion and captivity by the king of Assyria, many people will flee from the cities. Many people are doing and advocating this today in anticipation of bad times.

The Lord here uses the oak and terebinth trees as a metaphor to represent Israel. Throughout Isaiah, we read of the Oaks of Bashan and the Cedars of Lebanon which are both metaphors for Israel. The people of Israel, or the church, will be felled but a shoot will spring up and this represents those who will be redeemed, or the holy offspring. This is the righteous remnant and the group to which we want to belong. Those who either escape on the exodus or who survive the captivity will be gathered to Zion singing songs of joy.

During this period of 42 months of judgment on the world, the righteous and repentant people will gather to Zion amid the great destruction that is taking place in the world. Those on the exodus, the wise virgins who were prepared at the beginning of the tribulation, will escape to the wilderness for 42 months. The remainder of the church will have to suffer the tribulation or captivity of the beast during which many will die. In the end, though, all the righteous who survive this period will gather to Zion and there prepare for the Millennium.

The Two Witnesses

The two witnesses or two prophets are only mentioned in Revelation 11 by John. The entire chapter is a homogeneous unit with the parts interrelated so it is important to look at the revelation as a whole to get not only the setting but a couple of time checks. For this reason the entire chapter is quoted below with the verses numbered for reference:

> 1 And there was given me a reed like unto a rod: and the angel stood saying, Rise, and measure the temple of God, and the altar, and them that worship therein.
>
> 2 But the court which is without the temple leave out, and measure it not; for it is given unto the Gentiles: and the holy city shall they tread under foot forty and two months.
>
> 3 And I will give power unto my two witnesses, and they shall prophesy a thousand two hundred and threescore days, clothed in sackcloth.
>
> 4 These are the two olive trees, and the two candlesticks standing before the God of the earth.
>
> 5 And if any man will hurt them, fire proceedeth out of their mouth, and devoureth their enemies: and if any man will hurt them, he must in this manner be killed.
>
> 6 These have power to shut heaven, that it rain not in the days of their prophecy: and have power over waters to turn them to blood, and to smite the earth with all plagues, as often as they will.
>
> 7 And when they shall have finished their testimony, the beast that ascendeth out of the bottomless pit shall make war against them, and shall overcome them, and kill them.
>
> 8 And their dead bodies shall lie in the street of the great city, which spiritually is called Sodom and Egypt, where also our Lord was crucified.

9 And they of the people and kindreds and tongues and nations shall see their dead bodies three days and an half, and shall not suffer their dead bodies to be put in graves.
10 And they that dwell upon the earth shall rejoice over them, and make merry, and shall send gifts one to an other; because these two prophets tormented them that dwelt on the earth.
11 And after three days and an half the Spirit of life from God entered into them, and they stood upon their feet; and great fear fell upon them which saw them.
12 And they heard a great voice from heaven saying unto them, Come up hither. And they ascended up to heaven in a cloud; and their enemies beheld them.
13 And the same hour was there a great earthquake, and the tenth part of the city fell, and in the earthquake were slain of men seven thousand: and the remnant were affrighted, and gave glory to the God of heaven.
14 The second woe is past; and behold, the third woe cometh quickly.
15 And the seventh angel sounded; and there were great voices in heaven, saying, The kingdoms of this world are become the kingdoms of our Lord, and of his Christ; and he shall reign for ever and ever.
16 And the four and twenty elders, which sat before God on their seats, fell upon their faces, and worshipped God,
17 Saying, We give thee thanks, O Lord God Almighty, which art, and wast, and art to come; because thou hast taken to thee thy great power, and hast reigned.
18 And the nations were angry, and thy wrath is come, and the time of the dead, that they should be judged, and that thou shouldest give reward unto thy servants the prophets, and to the saints, and them that fear thy name, small and great; and shouldest destroy them which destroy the earth.
19 And the temple of God was opened in heaven, and there was seen in his temple the ark of his testament: and there were lightenings, and voices, and thunderings, and an earthquake, and great hail. (Rev 11:1-19)

In the first two verses, an angel gives John a measuring rod or reed to measure the temple. It is obvious that this temple is the one in Old Jerusalem which is made clear in verse two. We discussed these two verses in Chapter Two. One of the duties of the Davidic prophet/king is to rebuild the city and temple in troublous times (Dan 9:24-27). This takes place in the last 70 weeks of the tribulation or first 42 months when the king of Assyria conquers the world.

The symbolic giving of the reed to John signifies his last-days mission of directing the rebuilding of Jerusalem and the temple which he does in his role as the King of Israel. The Jews accept him as the Messiah before finally rejecting him because he preaches Christ to them. His rejection comes sometime in the last few of the seventy weeks. The seventy weeks end with the antichrist overrunning the city and the temple where he puts an end to the daily sacrifice. The abomination of desolation is then set up in the temple, which is the image of the beast. He will not tolerate the worship of any deity apart from himself. Since the Jews reject Christ, most also reject what remains of Judaism.

Today only a small percentage of Jews, 17 percent at the last poll, are religious. But of this number less than four percent are orthodox. The balance of religious Jews are liberal, reform or conservative. There are new branches of Judaism that have many members as well. Because religious Jews are a minority, there is beginning to be much reaction against them by secular Jews as they are called.

Last year in one of the new residential communities in Israel, a town called Tzoran east of the city of Netanya, there was great strife between the two and it continues. A Jewish religious school opened there in September 1998. But even before the school opened, there were protests and threats of violence if the school opened. In mid October a rally was held and the speaker called on the citizens of Tzoran "to expel the forces of darkness from their midst."

When the 25 six- and seven-year-olds arrived for the first day of school, they were met by a mob of about 60 adults who had brought attack dogs and tied them to the school gate. This continued for several months and at present the conflict continues. The protesters have virtually waged war on their religious neighbors. A pamphlet has circulated calling on the people to "enlist to defend the honor of man and his freedom." Signs have been placed throughout the community of which one reads, "Enough of religious coercion." The school has been repeatedly vandalized including tar having been poured over it. (*The Jerusalem Post*, March 19, 1999)

The war between secular and religious Jews continues in every aspect of life. In Jerusalem it has resulted in violent gang fights between secular and Haredi Jews. Many secular Jews consider the Haredim to be parasites who contribute little or nothing to the state and are a drain on resources. So we see Judaism being rejected by the Jews today and it is easy to see that at the time of the coming of the davidic king to the Jews, there will be few religious Jews there. Daniel tells us that many Jews take the part of the beast and raise a host, or army, against the daily sacrifice.

The armies of the antichrist have been kept at bay largely through the power of the Davidic King and when he is rejected, their protection ends temporarily. The army then enters the city and conquers it ending the daily sacrifice, as stated. The Davidic king is forced to leave.

In verse 2, the angel states that the holy city will be trodden "under foot forty and two months." Since this is the end of the first 42 months or the reign of the king of Assyria, the time remaining for the city to be trampled under foot, or occupied by enemies, is the judgment period which is also 42 months in duration.

Verse 3 continues from this point without any break with the Lord saying he will give power to his two witnesses, etc. So the two witnesses are commissioned at this midpoint period. When the Davidic prophet/king leaves Jerusalem, two other prophets are appointed to remain in the city for the last 42 months. These prophets are also empowered at the Council at Adam-ondi-Ahman and are very likely two of the 144,000 who are assigned to work with the remaining Jews in Jerusalem. They may be other Jews, however, called specifically for this very special mission.

This time identification is important because it confirms the order of events as depicted on the last-days chart at the end of this book.

Verse 5 shows us that they are translated beings who cannot be killed or hurt and if anyone tries to do so, he is killed by fire coming out of their mouths. This may be part of their power mentioned in verse 6 where it says that they have power over the elements which is the fulness of the priesthood. They can cause much havoc. They spend these 42 months preaching and calling the people to repentance but most of the people hate them.

Finally, the 42 month judgment period comes to an end and the final end of all people who have not been gathered is imminent. At the end of the period, the two witness are allowed to be killed. Verse 7 says that it is the beast from the bottomless pit, who is Satan and not the antichrist because he is long since dead (42 months ago). They are killed by the people and the invaders who are in Jerusalem still. John reminds us that this evil city is spiritual Sodom and Egypt where the Savior was crucified.

Verse 9 indicates that the city is still occupied by many tongues, kindreds and nations who shall see their bodies three days and a half but will not allow their bodies to be buried. The people will rejoice because they caused them much trouble. After the three days, they are resurrected and taken up to heaven. This causes the people to be astounded.

Things happen fast now because the end is near. It says that in that same hour they were taken up, a great earthquake destroyed the tenth part of the city killing 7000 people and now people start to take notice. They recognize the hand of God and give him glory or praise. John says that at this point the second woe is past, which you will recall was the loosing of the army of Lucifer upon the world to slaughter men for 13 months and a week. This is ended and the third woe is about to happen.

The third woe is the last battle when the Euphrates is dried up, which is the breaking of the power of the Jews and the kings of the east amass at Armageddon to come against the Jews in Jerusalem. This was covered earlier in this chapter.

So the mission of the two witnesses is the same as the other 144,000 except that they are to remain in Jerusalem and preach repentance. Those who repent will be gathered out to Zion or else left to be among the few survivors. There are not many left in Jerusalem at this time. The earthquake destroys a tenth of the city and 7000 people. If the earthquake also kills a tenth of the people, there are only about 70,000 remaining. This sounds about right.

Chapter V

The Last Days Time Line

One of the frequent criticisms of the outline of the last days in the foregoing chapters is the matter of time. We often hear the response that no one knows the hour nor the day of the Lord's coming. Gerald Lund, whose interesting presentations on the last days often received the same criticism, was wont to answer, "No one knows the hour nor the day of the Lord's coming but we know the month and the year." And while we are forced to agree that no one can tell exactly when he will descend in his glorious advent, he has given us much concerning the time sequence of the last days, along with a road map of events leading up to the advent. All we need to know is when the clock starts running, then all the following events will be pinpointed as to time.

As we discussed in the beginning of this book, members are looking for minor or inconsequential signs to occur before the bad times come. This, they believe, is the Lord's way of warning us so that when we see these signs, we will have ample time to put our houses in order and prepare "every needful thing." I have tried to show, however, that these little signs, as I call them, such as the missionaries being called home, missionary work starting among the Jews, three million people west of the Jordan River in Salt Lake Valley and the saints gathering to these mountains, Gospel to be taken to all nations, a work party sent to begin building the temple and Jackson County area, the US Constitution to hang by a thread, and many others, are not preliminary but occur, if at all, after the tribulation has already started. (The popular idea of a group being called to return to Jackson County to build the temple is pure myth and will not happen.) By then it will be too late.

The question we need to ask is, What will happen first? This is the thing we should be seeking if we are trying to unravel the mystery of the last days. A hint is given in the Lord's sermon to his disciples recorded in Matthew, Mark and Luke. The most often quoted is from Matthew 24. In that chapter the Lord cites several things that will happen in the last days in a random order. But starting with verse 36, he gives us an idea of conditions before his coming.

> *But of that day and hour knoweth no man, no, not the angels of heaven, but my Father only. But as the days of Noe were, so shall also the coming of the Son of man be. For as in the days that were before the flood they were eating and drinking, marrying and giving in marriage, until the day that Noe entered into the ark, And knew not until the flood came, and took them all away; so shall also the coming of the Son of man be....Watch therefore: for ye know not what hour your Lord doth come. But know this, that if the goodman of the house had known in what watch the thief would come, he would have watched, and would not have suffered his house to be broken up. Therefore be ye also ready: for in such an hour as ye think not the Son of man cometh.* (Matt 24:36-39, 42-44)

This is where we get the idea that no man knows the day and hour. But the verses following are to tell us how to know something about it and be ready. One thing is perplexing here, however. What he seems to be saying is that everything will be going along as normal and suddenly the Lord pops out of heaven and appears. We know from all the prophecies that this is not the way it happens. What about the antichrist, the captivity, the judgment and death of most of mankind? Something is not right here.

The problem is that what we conceive as the second coming and what the Lord means are two very different things. There is a strong indication that the Lord is not around right now. He seems to be somewhere doing something which we can only guess at, such as visiting someone else. He told us that he has cut off communication with the church today which we examined previously. In D&C, he said that we should call on him when he is near. He gave the parable of the man with the field who sends the workmen into the field and promises to visit the first in the first hour, the second in the second hour and so on. He ends by saying that we should call on him when he is near. (D&C 88:51-62)

He seems to refer to his coming to visit the earth in terms different than we do. And that is exactly what we find when we look at the many scriptures referring to his coming in the last days. We traditionally think only in terms of his glorious descent, but to him, this is only the final act in his great and marvelous last days work. His coming, then, is his coming to wreak vengeance on the world and prepare it for the millennial epoch. So in the above passage from Matthew when he says no man knows the day nor hour of his coming, he is talking about the beginning of the last days destruction and judgment, or specifically, the beginning of the tribulation. We quoted Isaiah 19 earlier where the prophet says "When the Lord enters Egypt riding on swift clouds…" (quoted below). This is what the Lord calls his coming. This is the day and hour we do not know. But he has given us some signs to know when it is near and this is what he was telling his disciples.

Now we have something to look for apart from the glorious descent which will happen too late to do anything about and the time of that event will not be important. In fact there will be no people around to see it except a handful of people in Jerusalem, if they are still there, and the remainder in New Jerusalem. The Savior will be among them and all the celestial people will be getting ready for the descent with him. There will be no mystery about it. The time will be known as well. All this puts us back to square one. The coming we need to know about is the coming he refers to and we find the answer in Isaiah, of course.

> *…When the Lord enters Egypt riding on swift clouds, the idols of Egypt will rock at his presence and the Egyptians' hearts melt within them. I will stir up the Egyptians against the Egyptians; they will fight brother against brother and neighbor against neighbor, city against city and state against state. Egypt's spirit shall be drained from within; I will frustrate their plans, and they will resort to the idols and to spiritists, to mediums and witchcraft. Then will I deliver the Egyptians into the hand of a cruel master; a harsh ruler will subject them, says my Lord, the Lord of Hosts.* (Isaiah 19:1-4)

The Lord also states in latter-day revelation:

> *Behold, vengeance cometh speedily upon the inhabitants of the earth, a day of wrath, a day of burning, a day of desolation, of weeping, of mourning, and of lamentation; and as a whirlwind it shall come upon all the face of the*

earth, saith the Lord. And upon my house shall it begin, and from my house shall it go forth, saith the Lord; (D&C 112:24-25)

The last days events begin with the circumstances described in Isaiah 19. The Lord will come to Egypt riding on swift clouds. This is what he refers to as his coming in Matthew 24 and elsewhere. This predates his glorious descent by more than seven years. The day and hour of this coming into Egypt is not known exactly but it is soon because all the signs of it are present. From a time perspective, since there are seven years of tribulation and judgment which occupy the last 42 months of the sixth seal and first 42 months of the seventh seal, there is not much room to slip the dates one way or another. The only ambiguity possible is that which may be due to our calendar versus the Lord's time reckoning.

We think our calendar is quite accurate but the seals are obviously not exactly 1000 years per our calendar. In addition there is a difference of opinion among scholars as to the exact date of birth of the Savior. The dates range from 6 BC to 8 AD and some are even outside these limits. In the church we have always accepted that the calendar date for the birth of the Savior is correct as far as the year is concerned. But this is not to say the Lord was born at the beginning of or that his birth was the beginning of the fifth seal.

The rise of the Church of Christ in these last days, being one thousand eight hundred and thirty years since the coming of our Lord and Savior Jesus Christ in the flesh, it being regularly organized and established...in the fourth month, and on the sixth day of the month which is called April— (D&C 20:1)

Joseph Smith said, as is recorded in the heading to the revelation, that the Lord gave this exact wording as written including the precise day of the anniversary of his birth. Therefore, if he was born exactly 1830 years before, it establishes the accuracy of our calendars and we are in the very last years of the sixth seal as this is being written. Talmage declares the position of the church with regard to this date:

We believe that Jesus Christ was born in Bethlehem of Judea, April 6, BC I. (James Talmage, *Jesus The Christ*, p 104)

Talmage also dedicates a chapter (op cit Chapter Six) to a discussion of the Meridian of Time. The only place the meridian of time is mentioned is in the Book of Moses (5:57; 6:57, 62; 7:46). Talmage explains the meaning of the phrase.

> *The term "meridian," as commonly used, conveys the thought of a principal division of time or space; thus we speak of the hours before the daily noon as ante-meridian (a.m.) and those after noon as post-meridian (p.m.). So the years and the centuries of human history are divided by the great event of the birth of Jesus Christ. The years preceding that epoch-making occurrence are now designated as time Before Christ (BC); while subsequent years are each specified as a certain Year of our Lord, or, as in the Latin tongue, Anno Domini (AD). Thus the world's chronology has been adjusted and systematized with reference to the time of the Savior's birth; and this method of reckoning is in use among all Christian nations.* (Talmage, op cit pp. 57-58)

Joseph asked the meaning of the seals in Revelation 7:2:

> Q. *What are we to understand by the book which John saw, which was sealed on the back with seven seals:*
>
> A. *We are to understand that it contains the revealed will, mysteries, and the works of God; the hidden things of his economy concerning this earth during the seven thousand years of its continuance, or its temporal existence.*
>
> Q. *What are we to understand by the seven seals with which it was sealed?*
>
> A. *We are to understand that the first seal contains the things of the first thousand years, and the second also of the second thousand years, and so on until the seventh.* (D&C 77:6-7)

These scriptures and comments are the facts upon which we have to base any time reckoning. In the Book of Moses, the Lord, or rather the Father who is speaking to Moses, uses the term "meridian of time" four times. This point in time is the dividing line between time periods rather than a time period itself. The time meridians on the earth are lines and not zones. The time zones are between the meridians. So the meridian of time, as Talmage states, is merely the line separating two time periods and is not of any measurable duration itself. This would seem to indicate that the meridian, the time line itself, was crossed with the birth of the Savior.

That being the case, the revelation by the Savior that the restoration of the church was exactly 1830 years from his birth, or from the meridian line in time, then we are, in fact, in the last years of the sixth seal. The only other ambiguity is whether or not the seal is exactly 1000 years. The only fact we have is D&C 77:6-7 above which states that the seals are 1000-year periods. The language is quite precise and there is no ambiguity or approximation. The Lord says the seals are 1000 years.

Based on the few revelations we have as cited above, we can assume that we are correct in our conclusion that the seals are very close to 1000 years each, that our calendar is correct and we are in the very last years of the sixth seal.

If the sixth seal coincided exactly with our calendar, then the sixth seal should end on December 31, 2000. The tribulation or reign of the antichrist takes place during the last 42 months of the sixth seal. That would have put the date for the beginning of the tribulation at July 1, 1997. Since that date has passed, we know that the Lord's reckoning is not the same as ours and he is not going by our calendar.

The calendar is much like a fuel gauge on a car. If our car will go about 300 miles on a tank of gas, then we know we can go that far. As we travel, the fuel gauge indicates approximately how much fuel we have remaining. When the car reaches 300 miles, the fuel gauge reads "Empty" but the car keeps going for some little distance yet. We are now running on empty and are at the end of the sixth seal. At the time of publication of this book we have passed the empty mark and are running out of time. The whirlwind is about to sweep down upon us and the time for preparation is all but past.

As mentioned above, the first events or signs will not be the conventional signs most members anticipate. The first thing to happen will be some catastrophe which comes upon the church. The Lord says it will begin upon his house. This is the church. In Isaiah 2:2 the Lord calls this nation the "mountain of the Lord's house."[illegible] His house is that part of Israel that is gathered here, or the church specifically, referring to the headquarters where the heads are. So some calamity will come upon the church as a whirlwind, meaning fast. At the same time, or immediately following, the civil war will begin in this country. The civil war will necessarily be quite brief but it will cause the country to be weakened to the point where a harsh ruler invades and conquers the country. This was discussed in Chapter One. These two acts are the first of the last-days signs.

When the captivity, or delivery of Egypt into the hands of the harsh ruler and cruel master, who is the king of Assyria, begins, the clock begins to run and we know with some precision when the other events take place as shown on the last days chart. The rise of the antichrist and invasion of the US is at 0 on the last days chart time line. It is at the left edge of the chart. All the other prophecies and signs take place after the invasion of the antichrist. Those who are waiting for the minor signs will be disappointed because then it will be too late. When the king of Assyria strikes, or rather, when the trouble begins in the US, the days of preparation are over. Those who are unprepared will remain so.

At the top of the last-days chart is a line divided into years and representing the last seven years of this dispensation or the last 42 months of the sixth and first 42 months of the seventh seal. The first half of the line is 1260 days or 42 months and begins when the king of Assyria takes power and invades the US and the world. The time for this is given in Revelation 12:6. Just after the invasion by the king of Assyria is a wide bar marked "Exodus." This is the exodus explained in detail in Chapter Two. The righteous remnant flees into the wilderness for 1260 days according to John. Isaiah describes the exodus also and reveals that it begins immediately after the invasion. Also in Revelation 12:5-6, the coming of the Davidic prophet is at the same time. As soon as he is delivered, the woman (the righteous remnant) flees into the wilderness (the exodus). Isaiah makes clear that the Davidic prophet/king arises at the same time as the antichrist.

The time from the from the rise of the antichrist to the center line is 42 months. John tells us in Rev 13:5 that "power was given him to continue forty and two months." After 42 months in power, he is destroyed by the Davidic king. Daniel explains that his destruction comes at the same time that the Ancient of Days sits, or the council at Adam-ondi-Ahman (7:9). He also states that the beast makes war with the saints and prevails against them until the great council (7:21-22, 25). This 42-month period is called the tribulation of the saints by the Lord in numerous places and takes place in the first 42 months which coincide with the reign of the antichrist.

The bottom wide bar represents the Jews in Jerusalem. Although it is not shown, the city of Jerusalem is under siege for 2300 days. The 2300 days is equal to six years and five months so Jerusalem is besieged and remains so for nearly the entire seven years of the tribulation and judgment. Even though the antichrist is destroyed after three and a half years, those who succeed him will still be at war and Jerusalem will still be under conquest.

In the lower wide bar near the center or end of the tribulation, there is a note about the 70 weeks. We discussed this in detail in Chapter Two. This is the period at the end of the 42-month tribulation. This was fully covered before but the coverage of this event is found in Daniel 9:24-27 and quoted below.

There are two times which are given by the angels speaking to Daniel. Daniel wants to know when these things he is being told will happen and how long they will last. In Chapter 12, Daniel is specifically asking about the time of the desolation. The angel tells him:

> *And from the time that the daily sacrifice shall be taken away, and the abomination that maketh desolate set up, there shall be a thousand two hundred and ninety days. Blessed is he that waiteth and cometh to the thousand three hundred and five and thirty days.* (Dan 12:11-12)

Daniel is told concerning the 70 weeks:

> *Know therefore and understand, that from the going forth of the commandment to restore and to build Jerusalem unto the Messiah the Prince shall be seven weeks, and threescore and two weeks: the street shall be built again and the wall, even in troublous times. And after threescore and two weeks shall Messiah be cut off, but not for himself: and the people of the prince that shall come shall destroy the city and the sanctuary; and the end thereof shall be with a flood, and unto the end of the war desolations are determined. And he shall confirm the covenant with many for one week: and in the midst of the week he*

shall cause the sacrifice and the oblation to cease, and for the overspreading of abominations he shall make it desolate, even until the consummation, and that determined shall be poured upon the desolate. (Dan 9:24-27)

So the commandment to build the street and the city is given to the Davidic king and it takes 69 weeks to accomplish the work while they are under siege by the antichrist. But after 62 weeks the Jews reject the Davidic prophet/king. He is obviously still around, however, because they have 70 weeks to repent. During one week near the end, he confirms the covenant with those who have accepted the Savior and the Davidic covenant. But when he is rejected, his protection is withdrawn and near the close of the 70 weeks, the antichrist enters the city, puts an end to the daily sacrifice and sets up his image in the temple, which is the abomination of desolation. The angel tells Daniel that from the time the daily sacrifice is stopped until the cleansing of the sanctuary and destruction of the invaders, will be 1290 days. So the daily sacrifice is taken away about 30 days before the end of the tribulation or about week 65 or 66 of the 70 weeks.

At the end of the book, however, in the penultimate verse, the angel adds without explanation, "Blessed is he that waiteth, and cometh to the thousand three hundred and five and thirty days." So the desolation will last 1290 days but blessed is he who survives 1335 days. What happens 45 days after the judgment ends? The only event that has not taken place is the formal Second Coming. By deduction, then, this has to be the time when the Savior will make his glorious advent.

Since the time given in the books of Revelation and Daniel are in days or months of 30 days, the time could be a little longer. We now have an average of thirty and a half days per month which adds between 35 and 40 days per seven years. With the periods of silence or peace, the additional days for our calendar and the 45 days indicated by the angel, it could affect the time for the glorious advent.

Regardless of the date it begins, we will know when it happens and then the other dates as shown on the chart will be known. The only date unknown at the moment is the 0 time line at the left. All the following events are measured in very precise terms in the scriptures as we have shown. The important concern is that it has to be very close because we are apparently in the final few months of the sixth seal. There is not much time to finish our preparations. We must expect the calamities to begin very soon. If we have a little extra time, a few more months to run on empty, that will be good. But in view of the facts shown in this work, are you willing to take the risk?

The last-days chart puts into time perspective all the major events of the last days. This is a valuable aid to understanding what have been confusing time periods. Biblical scholars have tried for years to give some other interpretation to the 1260 days, the 70 weeks and so on. Some have suggested that the 70 weeks are a prediction of the time of the coming of the Savior. This is Bruce McConkie's idea and is found in the heading of Daniel 9. This is ridiculous, of course, but such ideas have prevailed and since they are printed in the scriptures, though far from scripture themselves, they are sometimes given the same weight as the scriptures that follow.

Some have tried to convert the 1260 days of the woman fleeing into the wilderness to some number of years. Accepting the erroneous idea that the woman fleeing into the wilderness was the great apostasy, they try to plug the 1260 into a period between some obscure and meaningless events such as the time between the fall of the Roman Empire and the birth of some little known reformer 1260 years later. Such exercises have done nothing to enlighten but rather have added to the misunderstanding.

The simple fact is that the Lord is writing to ordinary people such as you and I. He does not expect us to figure out difficult mystical time schemes. When he says 1260 days and later 42 months describing the same period, it can only be literal, and we have shown that the literal times are reasonable and tie the last days events together into a logical pattern. All the scriptures agree and there is no confusion when we have the key. And while we cannot pinpoint the events to a day nor hour, we know they are close. The Lord has not hidden these things from us and has given us the means to decipher the scriptural code.

Chapter VI

Epilogue

This view of the major events of the last days drama has been given to put these events in perspective and establish a time line for their occurrence. The question remaining is, "What do I do now?"

The Lord gave the marvelous revelations that we have briefly reviewed for a single purpose. He wants his people to repent of the things he has condemned as presented in Isaiah. To encourage us to do this, he has described in explicit, graphic detail the death and unbearable plagues that are about to fall upon humanity and how the righteous of Israel can escape them.

I had read the Book of Mormon most of my life and had become familiar with the great saga presented therein. As I became more knowledgeable of the things in the book, I tried to pattern my life after the righteous men in those times. As with most of you, I had my heroes and thought that if I could live as these great men lived, I would come out okay in the sight of God.

At some point I read the commandment of the Lord in 3 Nephi 23 to search and study the Book of Isaiah. As far as I could find, it was the only book he specifically commanded us not only to read, but also to diligently search. Since this was the one thing I lacked to become "perfect," I began a diligent study of Isaiah. I soon found, however, as many of you have done, that the book was impossible to understand.

This led to great frustration. Here is a solemn commandment to search the book but it is written in archaic English whose words have different meanings today. It is difficult to wade through the language alone before one even gets to the original writing itself. I studied Elizabethan English, taking classes at the university and I enjoyed reading Shakespeare and the other great works of the period which are very important to me and I still read them, however, this did not unseal the book for me.

Over the years whenever a work on Isaiah would appear in the bookstores, I would buy it thinking that someone out there must know how to understand it. Over the years I bought every book I saw purporting to explain Isaiah. Each book I opened revealed the fact that none of the writers understood Isaiah either. The only book of any value was Skousen's *Isaiah Speaks to Modern Times* and this was not because he understood what Isaiah was saying to modern times, but because of his exhaustive research into the many names Isaiah uses. When you come to Kedar, for example, you only have to look up that name in Dr. Skousen's book and he explains who Kedar was. The only problem is that you still have to figure out what Kedar means because it is a metaphor as are nearly all the names and places in Isaiah.

Of course I was familiar with Nephi's complaint that his people could not understand Isaiah and the reason he gave was that they had not been taught after the manner of the teaching or the manner of prophesying among the Jews. It seems that there is a special metaphorical and hidden language the Hebrew prophets used and to understand what they were saying, one had to be taught this manner of speaking. Some even went to Rabbinic schools or hired rabbis to teach them such as Joseph Smith did. As he was preparing to translate the scriptures, he hired a Jewish scholar to teach him Hebrew and the manner of prophesying of the Jews. I also took classes in Hebrew but the language taught was modern Hebrew and was not of too much help.

One day in about 1983, I was in Deseret Book and noticed a little volume entitled *The Apocalyptic Book of Isaiah: A New Translation With Interpretive Key* by Avraham Gileadi. I, of course, purchased it and to my surprise I discovered that I could read it and understand the grammar and the literal meaning of the verses. I began to understand much of this book. I met Dr. Gileadi and was anxious to understand more because his interpretive key did not completely open the window of knowledge for me.

He began speaking at firesides and explaining his conversion to the church while he was a rabbinic student in Israel. In about 1988, his book was republished by Deseret Book but the introduction and explanation of how to interpret the metaphors and rhetorical links used by Isaiah were greatly expanded and made up about half the book. This second issue was called *The Book of Isaiah: A New Translation With Interpretive Keys From the Book of Mormon.* This book was a hot seller and became very popular among the people who study the scriptures seriously. This book was sold out and Deseret Book decided not to print any more even though it was a very popular and needed work.

It seems there was a controversy about some ideas that were now clear from the Book of Isaiah, especially about the Davidic prophet/king. The self-appointed guardians of the canon decided that they disagreed with this idea and labored to discredit Dr. Gileadi and his work. As a result, he was excommunicated for apostasy, which many witnesses and personal testimonials showed to be absolutely unjust. Later they started rumors that he had been guilty of some moral infractions which those of us who know him knew to be false. This was done to discredit one of the greatest scholars and righteous Latter-day Saints because he had unsealed this great and hidden book which Nephi said would come to light in the days the prophecies therein were about to be fulfilled.

Dr. Gileadi came to the church as another who is a type; Samuel the Lamanite. The Nephites found themselves in apostasy although Nephi, the prophet and head of the church was there presiding. Samuel was sent from the hated Lamanites by the Lord to call the people to repentance and announce certain events which were about to occur. He was a foreigner and they tried to kill him as he spoke from the wall of the city. When he had delivered his message, he left and was seen no more.

The Nephites and other leaders of the church totally neglected his words. They did not even write them down. When the resurrected Lord appeared to them over 40 years later he examined their records and asked where the words of Samuel were. Mormon records only, “And it came to pass that Nephi remembered that this thing had not been written.” (3 Nephi 23:12).

Avraham Gileadi was prepared by the Lord for many years to do this one thing; translate the book of Isaiah and teach the church the manner of prophesying of the Jews. The Lord brought him to Israel and he studied in the rabbinic schools learning the manner of writing of the Hebrew prophets. When the time was appropriate, someone handed him a Book of Mormon which he immediately recognized as Hebrew writing. He joined the church and came to this place.

Being moved upon by the Spirit of the Lord, he saw that no

one in the church could understand Isaiah so he set out, as he says, having the key of the manner of prophesying of the Jews and now the key of revelation which the church possessed, to translate the book. When it was done, it was shown to Isaiah scholars of the world who praised it generally as the best translation in existence. This same endorsement was given by LDS scholars including Dr. Hugh Nibley.

Thousands of people flocked to hear him give lectures and classes on the meaning of the book and the manner of interpreting it. The unsealing of the Book of Isaiah through the translation and interpretive explanations, opened the book to the understanding of thousands of people who had shared my frustration. The translation and information from this book have literally changed tens of thousands of lives and people have repented of idolatry, injustice and Sabbath breaking and have completed their preparations for the coming tribulation which Isaiah describes.

The unsealing of the Book of Isaiah has also opened other prophetic books to clear understanding such as Revelation and Daniel which, along with Isaiah, are the three most important prophetic books regarding the last days. It also opens up such books as Jeremiah, Ezekiel, Joel, Hosea and other Old Testament books which contain last days prophecies and which are also written in the Hebrew manner of prophesying. At last the prophetic books are opened to our understanding.

Many people said they still could not understand the new translation of Isaiah because it still took much study and effort to understand the metaphors and hidden meanings. For this reason some of Dr. Gileadi's students put together a work which is called *The Scriptures of the Last Days* containing the complete text of the Gileadi Isaiah and commentary from his lecture tapes. The work also contained a commentary on the books of Revelation and Daniel. This last work was distributed largely through the underground LDS market which allowed people to freely copy it and tens of thousands of copies were put into the hands of interested people. This work has been enlarged and edited and is now, at the time of this writing, about to be republished. This work contains the complete books of Isaiah, Revelation and most of Daniel with verse-by-verse commentary. In addition, the commentary contains many references to other prophecies and related topics. This is a most valuable reference work you must have if you are interested in these prophecies.

The injustice done Dr. Gileadi was rectified by his rebaptism into the church. In 1995, he published another work, *The Literary Message of Isaiah* which was published for general readership. The great value of this work is that Dr. Gileadi has highlighted the metaphors which relate to the Davidic prophet/king. In addition there is an exhaustive index listing every noun, verb and adjective. It is a valuable study resource as well.

These inspired works then have opened the eyes of those who have desired to know the things Isaiah says as well as obey the commandment of the Savior to search them diligently.

The Book of Isaiah, being an inspired prophetic book which the Lord has commanded us to study, like the Book of Mormon, has its power to convince the reader of its truth. When you read the book with a sincere desire to know, the Spirit will manifest the truth and will open your eyes to wondrous views. And if you are sincere, it will change your life and you will begin to rid yourself of idolatry, injustice, Sabbath breaking and procrastination in setting your house in order including your year supply of food and necessaries.

I am sure that as you read this work, you thought it was a little dogmatic. This was intentional. The commentaries in this book are not opinion except where stated, but are known truth and this book testifies of them. This is not a work written to get rich (who could get rich writing to such a limited audience?) nor to satisfy an enlarged ego. This work was hurriedly written to get this vital information to the righteous remnant so that they who are not quite prepared will know that time is short and to encourage them to make their final preparations.

This book is of no use to the skeptic or to the person who does not care. It is of no use to him who thinks he knows all about the last days because he can recite the Gospel Doctrine class myths about these times. He who has hardened his heart and will not accept any truth that is not written in the Sunday School manuals or other official places apart from the scriptures, will not accept anything we might say. This book will be of benefit only to those who know there will be a last days exodus and who long to be with the people who are there at the birth of Zion;

to those who know of and are waiting for the herald of the Lord, the Davidic prophet to reestablish the Kingdom of Israel; and to those who have wanted to know of these things but have not known where to go for the true answers. They are the wise virgins and to the small group of wise virgins, who take the Holy Spirit for their guide, these will be most valuable writings and may save the lives of some. This is my fervent hope.

About The Author

Robert Smith studied languages and historical linguistics at the University of Texas and the University of Utah, completing undergraduate and graduate degrees. In 1976 he completed his Ph.D. in historical linguistics. He has also done post-doctoral studies in Hebrew and Biblical Hebrew at the University of Utah and at Hebrew University in Jerusalem. He has taught at colleges in Utah and California.

For the past several years, he has been involved in research in Central and South American native languages—Quechua, Aymara, Proto Cholan and Nauatl. This research is identify the language families from which they came and to confirm their relation to Asian Semitic languages.

He is also doing new translations and commentaries on the Old Testament prophetic books. Volume I of a three-volume translation and commentary of the twelve prophets is nearing completion and should be published soon.

In 1992 he published a commentary on the books of Isaiah, Daniel, and Revelation entitled *Scriptures of the Last Days*; thousands of copies were sold to people interested in last-days prophecy. He is revising this book, currently out-of-print, and expects to publish an enlarged edition in late 1999. Many readers of that book asked Robert to write a summary of the major events covered in these three prophetic books and provide a chronological order of events to come. And thus he has written *The Last Days Unsealed.*

Robert is a lifelong member of The Church of Jesus Christ of Latter-day Saints and served two missions and in various ward and stake callings. He was born in Utah and lived most of his life there as he and his wife raised their seven children.